Poem on pg
124-125

Will I Ever Be Whole Again?

Will I Ever Be Whole Again?

Surviving the Death of Someone You Love

SANDRA PICKLESIMER ALDRICH

HOWARD®
PUBLISHING CO.

Our purpose at Howard Publishing is to:

- *Increase faith* in the hearts of growing Christians
- *Inspire holiness* in the lives of believers
- *Instill hope* in the hearts of struggling people everywhere

Because He's coming again!

Will I Ever Be Whole Again? © 1999 by Sandra P. Aldrich
All rights reserved. Printed in the United States of America
Published by Howard Publishing Co., Inc., 3117 North 7th Street, West Monroe,
Louisiana 71291-2227 in association with Alive Communications, Inc.,
1465 Kelly Johnson Blvd., Ste. 320, Colorado Springs, CO 80920.

99 00 01 02 03 04 05 06 07 08   10 9 8 7 6 5 4 3 2 1

Library of Congress Cataloging-in-Publication Data
Aldrich, Sandra Picklesimer.
    Will I ever be whole again? : surviving the death of someone you
love / Sandra Picklesimer Aldrich.
        p. cm.
    Includes bibliographical references.
    ISBN 1-58229-012-1
    1. Consolation. 2. Bereavement—Religious aspects—Christianity.
3. Grief—Religious aspects—Christianity. 4. Death—Religious
aspects—Christianity.   I. Title.
BV4905.2.A33   1999
248.8'66—dc21   99-19406
                                                                    CIP
Edited by Nancy Norris
Interior design by LinDee Loveland

The following publisher has generously given permission to use an extended quotation from a copyrighted work. From *A Mother's Grief Observed* ©1997. Used by permission of Tyndale House Publishers, Inc. All rights reserved. The following individuals/organizations have generously given permission to reprint poems and/or stories: The Compassionate Friends, Katie Troupe, Barbara Reynolds, and Trish Colby.

Scripture quotations not otherwise marked are from the New International Version, © 1973, 1978, 1984 by International Bible Society. Used by permission of Zondervan Bible Publishers. Other Scriptures are quoted from the King James Version (KJV), © 1961 by The National Publishing Co.

For my mother,

Wilma Farley Picklesimer

and

in memory of my father,

Mitchell Picklesimer Sr.

Contents

CONTENTS

Dear Reader,

The fact that you're holding this book undoubtedly means one of two things: You're trying to move through a recent grief, or you're wanting to help someone who is. My heart goes out to you on both counts. And if you're that rare person who is trying to understand the dynamics of grief without the personal experience, then I am indeed impressed. After all, most of us don't want to face the reality of death until we're forced to. Even now I cringe as I think of those high school students who sat in my classroom years ago, hurting after the death of someone close to them. But I didn't know how to comfort them. And with my school district's "no touching" policy, I couldn't offer any much-needed Kentucky hugs. (Richard and Ann, among others, please forgive me. I trust someone helped you through that awful time of losing your beloved stepmother and father.) It took my young husband's death to open my eyes to the need of human comfort through a soft word or a hug.

But even though we, as a society, often don't know how to comfort, the statistics are rather clear: Ten out of every ten people who are born into this life will die. Growth ends in death—at one time or another. And no matter how great our world's scientific advancements to prolong life, we can't stop the ultimate result—death. It's like Senator John Glenn said to the media in the spring of 1998: "There's still no cure for the common birthday."

So as you read the following pages, know that they've been written by someone who understands grief and its impact only too well. Much of this material appeared in my previously published book *Living through the Loss of Someone You Love*. In this edition, though, I've condensed the story of our battle with my thirty-eight-year-old husband's brain cancer and expanded the principles that can help others better understand grief. In this book, the first two chapters retell the battle that my young husband and I waged as cancer invaded his brain and our lives. When Don died after sixteen months, I was left to raise a ten-year-old son and an eight-year-old daughter.

The rest of the chapters deal with the principles of grief. If we understand what is happening to us, we can better deal with it. These principles will not only help you understand your own pain but will teach you how to help others who are experiencing grief. A couple of years after Don's death, I had the privilege of working at the R. G. and G. R. Harris Funeral Homes in the Detroit area as the community service director. During that time, I gave seminars with Dr. John Canine, who helped me understand grief in a new way and helped me see that this was a journey that could be walked.

At the end of the book, you'll find a Study Guide for each chapter, intended for group discussion or personal reflection to help you work through and understand the process of grief and loss.

So, come along, let me escort you through these pages. And may you know that you are not alone.

Sandra Picklesimer Aldrich

1 Clowns Aren't Supposed to Die

Facing the Reality of Death

The emergency-room doctor used such terms as "multiple lesions" and "metastasis" as he pointed to the numerous white spots on the CAT scan plates. Translated, the words meant Don's cancer was back. And this time it was in his brain.

I saw only sadness in the doctor's eyes. "Are you all right?" he quietly asked.

I forced myself to appear calm. "Yes, I'm all right for *now*. But you must tell me exactly what we're dealing with."

He looked at me for a long moment, then said, "Mrs. Aldrich, it's a Clark Four. That means it's advanced to the worst level."

Worst level? I was having trouble sorting his words. Less than four years earlier, when Don had a simple malignant melanoma removed from his shoulder, his doctor said he had nothing more to worry about.

I leaned forward, wishing I could pinch my leg to wake myself from this terrible dream. "So what can we *do?*" I asked.

"For now, we'll try to get the brain swelling down and make him comfortable. You said you're from the Detroit area? We can make arrangements to get Mr. Aldrich into the University of Michigan Hospital. It's imperative treatments begin soon."

Imperative? Why was my brain working so slowly?

I had to ask the dreaded question. "How much time do you think we have?"

"Metastatic brain lesions—especially of this multitude—grow very rapidly. It could be a matter of months, or perhaps only weeks. And you must know this cancer doesn't normally respond to treatment."

Doesn't normally respond? I thought of Don lying in a nearby darkened cubicle. I tried to keep panic out of my voice. "Are you saying our one hope is a miracle?"

He breathed out through his mouth and then nodded. "I'm sorry. I'm so very sorry."

The doctor and I silently walked toward the striped curtain where Don waited. My thoughts bumped against one another. Don couldn't die. He was too young. And he liked to laugh too much. Only philosophical old men were supposed to be handed news like this. Clowns were supposed to live forever.

What were Jay and Holly going to do without their daddy? He was their favorite parent...and they were only eight and seven. They needed him. I needed him! Oh, God, *please don't turn me into a widow.*

Widow. What a strange word. This meant I was going to be part of that sad, silent group at church. *I don't want to be a widow! I want to be Don's wife.*

The doctor pulled back the curtain.

Don was lying still, his right arm over his eyes, his left one hooked to the IV dripping morphine-based medicine into his vein.

I hurried over to my big, blond Scotsman and gently cupped my hand around his close-trimmed beard.

"Donnie?"

His answering "Hmmmm?" sounded as though it was coming from the bottom of a well. He struggled to open his eyes. Normally their deep blue color sparkled with some new joke. Now they were filled only with pain.

I took his hand, and together we listened to the doctor's comparison of the cancer to shards of broken glass scattered throughout his brain. The condition was inoperable.

After Don was admitted to the oncology ward, numerous medical specialists stopped by to shine their lights into his eyes before conferring together. Finally he was allowed to nap, so I gently kissed him good-bye, promising to return after I had told everyone the news. How I dreaded those calls. How could I tell his dad the cancer was back? Don's mother had died from cancer a few years earlier. Hadn't we had enough for one family?

How could I tell my parents? Don had always teased me, saying that if I ever left him, he was going home to live with my mother. And they loved him just as much as he loved them.

My thoughts kept turning to Jay and Holly. I dreaded telling them most of all. They always argued over whose turn it was to sit next to Don in the restaurants. How could I tell them the doctors were saying their daddy was going to die?

Twenty minutes later, after collecting Jay and Holly from the neighbors', I sat on a low stool facing them as they sat on the sofa, their feet not long enough to touch the floor. I took their little hands into mine. Don and I had agreed this was going to be their battle, too, so it was important to be honest with them right from the start.

They waited, all summer-tanned and blond, watching my face. Finally, as simply as I could, I told them about the new cancer.

Jay, the eight-year-old miniature of his father, stared at me. "Is he going to die?" he asked.

Suddenly hot tears were running down my cheeks again. "The doctor says he's going to."

Little Holly's eyes were wide. "Does God love Daddy?"

I stood up to get a tissue. "Of course He loves him. Very much."

Then she dropped a theological bomb: "If God loves Daddy, won't He make him well?"

I tried to explain that while God *could* heal their daddy, He might allow something else to happen. I also stressed that the Lord was with us, and that none of us was being punished for being bad. I'm not sure I covered all the important points though: I'd never had to explain God's sovereignty to a seven- and eight-year-old before. I had no greater understanding than my children. After all, why *does* God sometimes allow bad things to happen if He truly is in charge? I didn't realize that this area would be one that I would struggle with again and again in the days ahead.

Finally I suggested we pray. Jay began, his voice quivering. "Please, God, don't let my daddy die!"

Suddenly all I could do was hug them and cry. How small I felt.

After another trip to the hospital that evening, I slept fitfully. The next morning as I prepared breakfast for Jay and Holly, I told them about the day's scheduled bone and liver scans, but inwardly I was try-ing to comprehend life without the one who had filled my life for more than fifteen years. What would it be like to have only the three of us around the table like this?

And what if I never heard Don's booming laugh again? I first heard it after an InterVarsity meeting at college. Smiling, I had turned toward the sound, determined to find the possessor of such joy. As our relationship grew, I found that he met life's challenges with that same sense of humor, sometimes to my irritation. Now we were being asked to face our greatest crisis yet, one that couldn't be dismissed with a joke.

After leaving Jay and Holly with our neighbors again, I drove to the hospital. Don was propped up in the bed, the IV board still taped to his hand. I kissed him in greeting, and then asked if the doctor had been in, if his headaches were better, if he'd had a comfortable night. He had just as many questions for me—who was keeping the kiddos, had I called our friends?

Included in my report was my call to Marta Gabre-Tsadick. In helping her write her book about her family's escape from Ethiopia during the Marxist years, I had found my life profoundly affected. Don shook his head when I told him I planned to set the writing project aside.

"No. I want to see the book finished. In fact, I want to see two things finished: the book and the Pharaoh."

The Pharaoh was an intricate needlepoint wall hanging he had purchased because of the Egyptian material I included in my high-school mythology classes. It had become a family joke, though, as I ripped out almost as many crooked stitches as I put in. Don already had a spot in our living room picked out for the prize hanging, so I had kept poking the threads through the canvas.

Don studied me for several moments, his expression a mixture of amusement and Scottish fight. "San, remember I'm not dead yet. You've been working on both of them forever. I want to see them finished."

I could do nothing but agree.

The next morning, Jay insisted God wasn't going to let his daddy die. I certainly didn't want to discredit so great a faith, but I also knew too many cases where faith and denial had gotten confused, robbing the participants of saying important things while they still had opportunities. I didn't want our children to chant, "Daddy's going to die," but I knew the danger of expecting God to perform His miracles *our* way.

Then I remembered Corrie ten Boom's illustration with her needlepoint at the end of the movie *The Hiding Place*. She had first shown the tangled underside, explaining that it represented our limited vision here on earth. She then turned it over to show a golden woolen crown, explaining that the threads woven together produced the perfect result that is seen from heaven's vantage point—the crown of His glory.

On Wednesday morning, I spread the Pharaoh needlepoint upside down on my lap and called Jay to me. All summer he had watched as I put in the stitches and yanked several others out. He delighted in watching the pattern take a recognizable shape. I sent up a quick prayer before I spoke.

"Jay, look at all these tangled threads. It looks like one big mess, huh?"

He nodded, so I continued. "Well, life is often like that. All we see now is the mess. Often the dark colors overwhelm the light colors, just like these do. But when we get to heaven, look what happens."

6

I turned the needlepoint over. "See? When we get to heaven we'll see exactly what the Lord was doing. And we'll know it wasn't a mess after all. And that's how it is with your daddy's illness."

Jay stared at the intricate pattern. When he turned back to me, his eyes were bright. "And you know what, Mom? I'll bet the colors God uses are beautiful ones we never see on earth either."

He leaned against me as I put my arm around him.

Holly's acceptance of the problem wasn't so easily solved. She had retreated into babyish behavior. She even started sucking her thumb at night, something she had given up years earlier. When she visited her dad at the hospital, she was fine. But at home, she whined. I had little energy, so all I could do was give her extra hugs and let her sit on my lap whenever she wanted. If I was having a rough time understanding this, how could I expect a child to?

Throughout our marriage, Don and I had been content with the traditional roles—he the protector, me the nurturer. But now our roles were reversing, and it was up to me now to protect Don. I met with the doctors, questioned each new medical test, and made all the decisions. I didn't relish my new role, but I had no choice but to stagger on.

During the evening of the last day of tests, Jay and Holly were to sing in a musical program at the lake where we had our summer home, so the three of us left the hospital early. As the children and I arrived at the community lodge that served our close-knit neighborhood, a friend asked about our plans to return to the hospital in the Detroit area the next morning. Suddenly the tears were threatening to stream down my face, so I stammered, "I'm sorry, but I'm just so tired." *Tired* didn't begin to describe the pain I felt as I thought of losing Don, but I couldn't verbalize that as I foolishly tried to be brave. How nice it would have been if she had put her arms around me and said it was okay to hurt—or better still, hugged me and cried with me. Instead she nodded and said, "Well, you're only human." *Human* was exactly what I didn't want to be.

As we entered the dining area of the lodge, several friends insisted I join them for a cup of tea. Others stopped by to remind me of their prayers. One friend patted my arm as she encouraged, "You and Don are such wonderful Christians. I just know God is going to heal him."

I couldn't answer as the tears finally spilled onto my cheeks. She didn't know us well after all. If Don's healing depended on *our* goodness, we had no hope.

The next morning, Don was transferred to the University of Michigan Hospital, which was closer to our home in southeast Michigan.

In a teaching hospital, Don was merely an interesting terminal case to many of the medical students. I wanted to shake their instructors as they dispassionately read the charts aloud or held up the latest CAT scans.

"Look at him!" I wanted to shout. "He's not just a 'thirty-eight-year-old, Caucasian male with multiple metastatic lesions to the brain. Malignant melanoma.' He's a good husband and daddy who loves the Lord. He's a loyal U of M football fan! His favorite vacation day is golf in the morning and tennis in the afternoon. Look at him!"

Of course I never shouted those things, but I stared at the students, willing them to look at our faces. Don handled the same discomfort by speaking directly to them, sometimes asking a question, sometimes teasing the examiner about cold hands. Undoubtedly, the students' distance was emotional protection. Maybe most didn't know how to respond, so they hid behind their concept of "professionalism."

One of the students though, Mr. Nelson, smiled at us directly. We had met him when he took Don's medical history during the admission procedure.

As he asked about major illnesses of other family members, I opened the canvas bag that I now carried constantly. Don grinned as I untangled more threads, so I held up the Pharaoh for him to see the progress.

Then as he answered Mr. Nelson's questions, I occasionally corrected him: "Honey, your grandma had cancer too. Remember? It was in the twenties just after their visit to Scotland." Or "Wait, your brother had kidney stones a couple of years ago."

Finally Mr. Nelson turned to me apologetically. "Mrs. Aldrich, it's important that Mr. Aldrich answer these questions. We need to see how much of his normal brain function has been impaired by the lesions."

Properly chastened, I gave a startled "I'm sorry" and turned back to the Pharaoh.

Don chuckled. "But this is 'normal brain function' for me," he said. "San's always kept track of the family news. She sends the birthday cards and at reunions reminds me which of my cousins are divorced, so I don't ask about the wrong spouse. If you want my family history, you have to talk to her."

I smiled at my bearded Scotsman, grateful for his defense. But I bent over the needlepoint as Mr. Nelson continued the questions. The black border around the Pharaoh had given me trouble all summer, so I was anxious to finish it. Then, just as I was ready to connect the sides, I realized I had miscounted the canvas spaces. Groan. It would do no good to pull out those hundreds of stitches; much of the background was already completed. My choices were limited. I could abandon this whole project and go back to my quilting, or I could adjust the stitches and accept the obvious zigzag that would result.

I glanced at Don as he answered medical questions. How appropriate that I discovered the mistake right then—with him in blue pajamas on top of a white hospital sheet. The needlepoint imperfection was just a tiny reminder of what we were facing in our personal lives. We could give up, saying it was hopeless. Or we could make the necessary adjustments and allow the Lord to create something beautiful out of the imperfect zigzag in our lives. I touched the black, broken line in the pattern and spoke to God in my heart. *Create Your beauty, Lord. I trust You to bring Your good out of this trauma.*

During Don's stay at the University of Michigan Hospital, my parents took care of Jay and Holly to free me to spend my days at the hospital. Each night, I drove the fifteen miles from the hospital to my parents' home. They knew I would want Jay and Holly close to me at night, so they had set up two cots near the small iron bed that had been mine before I married.

That first night in my old moonlit room, I sat on the edge of the bed, listening to the soft breathing of my children. The stately pine trees planted at the turn of the century still shielded the windows. The wallpaper was the same too. I studied its lavender flowers, remembering my delight at the choice when our family moved in during my senior year in high school.

Suddenly I covered my face with my hands, reluctant to face this night in my old room. The last time I had slept in that room had been fifteen years earlier—the night before Don and I were married. That long-ago night, I'd had trouble getting to sleep as I wondered what it would be like to be a wife. Tonight I would wonder what it would be like to be a widow.

Radiation and chemotherapy treatments followed after Don was released from the hospital. Then he developed painful herpes zoster, commonly called *shingles*. His immune system was shot, and the specialized creams for the painful eruptions had not yet been developed. The doctors said all we could do was let them run their course. I wish I'd known back then about the importance of increasing vitamin B and dripping the oil from an opened vitamin E capsule over the open blisters. Maybe we could have eased the terrible pain caused by the exposed nerve endings. But we foolishly listened to the doctors who said nothing could be done.

During this time a friend from Nashville sent Don a card ending with, "I think it stinks you have shingles on top of everything else!" Don and I laughed aloud. We knew it stunk, too, but thought it was unchristian to voice that. I constantly struggled with what my proper attitude should be. I wanted so much for others to see God's reality and His comfort even in the midst of trauma, but we never seemed to get a break from the ongoing struggle.

Don had insisted I teach that fall, saying it was important to him to have at least one of us involved in "normal" activities each day. Reluctantly I returned to my classroom, but that autumn my faith struggle deepened. October's CAT scan showed that Don's cancer was still very much there. The doctor stressed that the lesions hadn't grown, but I wanted them *gone!* Hadn't Don been prayed over and for? Weren't we trying to do everything we possibly could—limiting red meats, increasing whole grains, taking a handful of vitamins each day? Yet nothing was working.

Don couldn't even enjoy the beautiful autumn that people said we were having. I saw it only to or from school, but I longed to be outside with our usual activities—cider mills, antique shows, and walks in the woods. But all of us were housebound.

Late one afternoon I stood at the front door, my arms filled with laundry, just as my neighbor's husband bounded into his car, tennis racket in hand. Jealousy seized me. Then I remembered a magazine story of a cat close to death after being hit by a car. The parents wanted their son to accept the cat's fate, but he insisted upon praying. The cat got well. Now my anger tumbled out.

"Okay, God, so why did you heal that cat and not Don?"

I didn't expect any answer, I just wanted to let God know I thought the whole situation was stinky—not just the shingles. Aloud, I listed all of the frustrations of the past few weeks, ending with not being able to be outside on such a beautiful day.

When I finally paused for breath, I waited, almost daring Him to answer. But instead of a rebuttal came peace—as though Someone were saying, "I *am* here."

That wasn't the answer I wanted, but if I believed God was sovereign, I had to accept it. If I'd trusted Him during the happy times, I had to trust Him in the valley. But one thing was still in my control— I could insist we all go to the park.

At my announcement of a picnic supper, Jay gave me a high-five and Holly squealed her delight, but Don balked. It was only when he saw the children's excitement that he set his jaw and pulled himself out of his orange chair. "I guess I can be as uncomfortable there as I am here."

At the park, Jay and Holly sprinted for the swings. I didn't want Don, who had always been active in sports, watching healthy bodies on the nearby soccer field, so I motioned toward the path leading to a stand of trees. He leaned heavily against me as he eased to the ground beneath the largest tree. We could hear the excited calls from the soccer game.

His head was down; he was undoubtedly hearing those same happy sounds. I wanted to call him back to me. "Don, look! We're sitting under a hickory tree."

I spotted empty hulls in the short grass. "I guess the squirrels beat us to them this year. We'll have to remember to come here early next year."

He glanced at me at the words *next year* but made no comment. Why hadn't I grabbed my Bible before we came here? Reading the Psalms always helped both of us. King David had expressed his own heart, surely never dreaming his words would encourage countless readers. I'd wanted our experience to bring some glory to our Father, too, but there we were sitting miserably under a hickory tree. Wouldn't the Lord be better glorified through Don's healing? I decided to tackle this issue head-on. I tried again.

"Donnie, please talk to me. I'm upset God hasn't healed you *our* way. I'm angry the CAT scan showed the same old lesions. I wanted this to be a testimony to God's healing power. But He's doing it His way, not mine, and I'm struggling with that."

The soccer crowd was cheering again. Don gestured that he wanted to stand up. "I know, San. I don't try to make sense out of this anymore. I know one thing though; I've got to get back to teaching. This sitting around counting the minutes is making me stir-crazy. I'm going to stop asking the Lord to take away this pain. I'm just going to ask Him to help me bear it."

Don had been teaching high school for sixteen years. So that week he persuaded his doctor to let him return to the classroom for a few hours each afternoon. Don may have convinced himself that he was handling the situation satisfactorily, but I wasn't sleeping much. The stress was building.

One morning, I left for school in a dense late-autumn fog. The air was so murky that I had to drive by instinct on the back road. After several moments of the car's crawling pace, I knew the stop sign should be just ahead. Ah, there it was.

As the car edged forward, I decided the fog wouldn't be as dense on top of the overpass. I inched to the top, expecting only greater visibility. Instead I was treated to an incredible sight. The little valleys surrounding the expressway were filled with pink mist rather than depressing, murky fog. And above the mysterious haze were the sun's rays, showing through purple and orange clouds. I gasped at the incredible beauty while the cars on the road below crept through the murk I had just escaped. If only they could have this view!

Even though I reentered the fog, the memory of the breathtaking vista buoyed my spirits. I continued toward school, strangely refreshed. Beauty would come after our personal fog too. We just hadn't arrived at a place where we could see above it.

The holidays that year were filled with the joy of being together. I tried not to dwell on how different Christmas would have been if the doctors had been right in their earlier assessment that Don would die within a few weeks. After Christmas, the cold winter days fell into manageable patterns, even though Don's shingles had deepened into "postherpetic neurology." He started calling the pain his "little man with a pitchfork."

But the remarkable news came in March—the CAT scan was

clear! I turned to the doctor and asked, "That means he's through with chemotherapy, right?"

Apologetically, he shook his head. The treatments had to continue to rid his body of other cancer cells undoubtedly lurking within Don's system.

Our struggle would continue.

The next week, the father of one of our friends died. His lung cancer supposedly had been mild, and the doctors told him he would live to be an old man. Instead he had heard only the word *cancer* and had given up.

Now I had a new emotional struggle as I wondered where the direct touch of the Lord stops—or begins—and where the individual's courage takes over. Why had Don's severe cancer gone into remission, while this man's supposedly mild form proved fatal? What part did prayer play in all of this? Can prayer change God's mind? I clung to my feeble faith for the days ahead. For now we would enjoy that delicious word *remission*.

Simple Reminders

1. Our brains often move slowly as we try to absorb bad news.

2. Children are affected by the trauma, too, and should be informed simply and lovingly about the situation from the beginning.

3. Young children need to hear that disease is not God's punishment for "being bad."

4. Life is often like the underside of a tapestry: All we see are the tangled, knotted threads.

5. The greatest beauty can come after the deepest personal fog.

2 *"Donnie, You're Free!"*

The Dreaded Outcome

With remission came a sweet "second chance" at life. As soon as school was out in June, we were delighted to pack for our summer place. And Don was able to return to the tennis court. Oh, his side still hurt from the shingles' aftermath, but he would set his jaw, determined to push aside the pain.

He was so confident about his restored health that he even insisted on removing himself from the hateful chemotherapy since two more CAT scans had shown no tumors. That autumn was filled with family outings again, even picnics at our hickory-nut park.

On the afternoon of Jay's tenth birthday in early October, Don came home for the celebration with a second-place trophy from the annual teachers' tennis tournament at his school. I yelped with delight, but he shook his head.

"I should have won first place. I must have pulled a muscle that slowed me down."

My mind refused to register the comment about the muscle. "Don! This time last year, the doctors were waiting for you to die. You're complaining because you took *second* place in a tournament this year!"

He grinned. "Hey, when you're used to being number one, it's hard to settle for second. What are you serving for Jay's party?"

The weeks that followed were wonderfully filled with our old activities. Then Thanksgiving arrived. That holiday meal had always been Don's favorite, so I spared no effort. We always had a twenty-two-pound turkey with the traditional dishes and invited as many relatives as we could crowd into our home.

The day was just as perfect as we had planned. Even though Don had mentioned that his legs hurt from all of his sports, we'd ignored the warnings. After all, he'd just been to our family doctor, who had taken x-rays. When nothing showed up, he gave Don muscle relaxants, saying his legs had been overcompensating for the pain in his side. Besides, he was scheduled for a thorough examination in January with his U of M oncologist. This could wait, Don said.

Now with Don sitting in front of a perfectly cooked turkey, I couldn't believe anything could be wrong. His blond hair was growing back, and his beard was as full as ever. In his beige sweater, he looked especially handsome as his banter kept the laughter crossing from table to table. Several relatives commented on how well he looked, adding they hadn't thought he'd live to see another Thanksgiving. I tried not to hear that.

Then as I outwardly went through the busy days before Christmas, the great "what-ifs" loomed. What if the cancer was out of remission? What if Don died?

While I struggled with new emotional battles, John Sherrill, my editor, called to give me a status report on Marta's book that I had finally finished and to check on Don. As I told him about the leg pain, I poured out my frustration.

"Just about the time I start to get on top of this, fear comes sweeping in," I said. "Then the battle begins all over again. I want so much for my Christian walk to be just that. But it's always a struggle with me."

John chuckled. "Who told you it's supposed to be a walk? It's a slugfest! Don's fortunate to have you as a warrior by his side. While he's battling the pain, you're battling on a different level."

I'd never thought of myself as a *spiritual* warrior, but I hugged his encouragement to me.

I had started taking the Pharaoh needlepoint to school so I could work on it for a few minutes during lunch. Each noon, I'd prop my Bible open on my desk, position the needle, and read the next verse as I pulled the thread through. But on the Monday after John called, as I read Ephesians, I realized that verse after verse was warning me of battle. Don's cancer *was* back! I dropped the needlepoint and sobbed.

School couldn't be over fast enough that day. Why had we been so blind? Why wouldn't we face what we knew?

When I arrived at Don's school to pick him up, I greeted him with, "We have to go to the hospital."

He nodded. "I know. Today my feet are wooden, just like last fall. I'll call my doctor as soon as we get home."

While he described the pain to the oncologist, I arranged for Jay and Holly to stay with neighbors. Then just before we left, the four of us stood by our front door and joined hands for our customary family prayer. Don was the sick one; I should have been the one to pray. But I shook my head sorrowfully as I looked at him. If I spoke, I'd lose what little stamina I had.

I marveled that Don's voice didn't crack. "Well, here we go again, Lord," he began. "Please be with us. Protect Jay and Holly and keep San strong. And please give me courage."

I drove to the hospital while Don rubbed his legs. His cane, once discarded, now rested against his knee.

"San, all day I've thought what would happen if I have to be in a wheelchair the rest of my life. Maybe we'll have to buy a van with one of those special lifts."

I offered quick encouragement. "Now aren't you glad you didn't marry a Size Three? I'll lug you all over the United States, if you want."

He grinned as he patted my ample thigh. "Yep. You always said I had to have the biggest and best."

Of course the medical tests that night confirmed the presence of the cancer we had tried to deny. And this time it was also in his spinal fluid. The doctors decided they'd begin with the standard chemotherapy since it apparently had worked before. We hoped the treatments would take care of both the brain lesions and the spinal fluid cancer. I kept remembering Don's comment about being in a wheelchair.

Just before they started the IV, Don pulled me close to him. "Just remember, San," he said. "The Lord never promised to give us an easy road, but He did promise to always be with us on that road."

In the days ahead, I would hold on to that statement.

One oncology team decided to do a lumbar puncture to draw spinal fluid and replace it with the same amount of chemotherapy. The resident doctor asked me to step outside the room.

I looked directly at him. "No. I'm going to sit in this corner and work on my needlepoint. And when you see my head down, ignore me. I won't be passed out; I'll be praying."

He moved toward the bed without another word.

For twenty minutes or more I silently prayed as the resident and intern made repeated attempts to find the spot between the vertebrae where the needle had to go. But Don's pain in his side didn't permit him to pull his body into the proper curl position. With each of his low moans, my stomach tightened that much more. Finally I stood up and faced the young men.

"Okay, I've had it. Now you *better* let me help. I'm through listening to you hurt him."

The resident glanced at the intern. Was he thinking of hospital regulations? Finally he spoke. "All right. Maybe if you pulled him into a tight curl. His spine has just enough curvature to make it difficult to insert the needle properly."

I leaned down and kissed Don's perspiration-soaked cheek.

"Come on, Donnie. We'll do it this time."

My right arm went around his shoulders, my left one under his knees. Bracing my legs against the bed, I pulled with all my Kentucky might.

"That's it! Now hold him just like that," the resident said.

For an eternity neither of us moved. Every fiber in my shoulders screamed for release. *If only I could move just a little. . . no, just a few more minutes.*

With my mouth close to Don's ear, I whispered prayers. "Thank You, Lord, for being with us. Thank You for the goodness You will bring out of this."

Somehow the minutes passed, and he was allowed to uncurl. Both the resident and intern nodded their thanks to me.

The next morning, I was back at the hospital by 7:30. Just as I turned the corner to Don's room, he was coming out of his cubicle—seated in a wheelchair! The very thing we had dreaded was now a reality. But none of that mattered as I saw the grin on my Scotsman's face.

"Oh, San! I'm glad you're here," he said. "You can help me bathe."

I leaned over to kiss him. "Okay," I said, "but I get to drive."

As I pushed the wheelchair, Don turned to look up at me. "You know, this isn't going to be so bad after all."

Looking down to smile at him, I turned the corner too sharply. The wheel caught, slamming the chair into the wall.

I gasped, but Don chuckled. "Maybe I'd better rephrase that."

In the middle of the hospital hall, I threw my arms around his shoulders and kissed the top of his head. Together we laughed with the joy of being together. Wheelchairs no longer mattered.

Additional lumbar punctures followed during the next few days. Apparently the resident had made a notation in Don's chart that I be allowed to help because even the new interns waited for me to take my position before beginning the procedure.

I always prayed in his ear to take our minds off of our separate pains, but at one point my shoulder muscles were burning so badly I had to stop to take a breath. As I did I realized that my dear husband was singing ever so softly, "What a friend we have in Jesus, all our sins and griefs to bear. What a privilege to carry everything to God in prayer."

I tried to keep my tears from falling on his face, but I knew the scene would stay in my heart forever.

Miraculously he improved enough to go home for three days beginning on Christmas Eve. That night, Don read the Christmas story in Luke 2 and then read chapter after chapter of the continuing story as Jay and Holly leaned against his good side. If anyone had looked through the window, he would have seen the Perfect Family, reading the Perfect Story in front of the Perfect Tree. But that was merely the image. We wanted nothing more than to remain together.

The next morning we were up before sunrise opening presents. As usual, Don and I delighted in watching the children open their packages before we exchanged our own gifts. When he finally unwrapped the ID bracelet I'd purchased several weeks earlier as a last-minute gift, he beamed. "San! I've always wanted one of these! Thanks."

As he turned to adjust the chain, I sighed. Married almost seventeen years and I'd never known he'd wanted an ID bracelet? What treasury of his thoughts and dreams were the children and I about to lose? But I shook off the depressing thoughts. The doctors would have a new method waiting for us in a couple of days. We'd lick this problem yet—and be better people because of the experience. My jaw tightened with the determination to think only positive thoughts.

Shortly, my family arrived. Then friends stopped by while the phone rang constantly. What a wonderfully zany day it was. And Don loved every minute.

Our time together went all too quickly, but it gave me enough time to see changes in Don's personality. He had always been boisterous, but now he was withdrawn, and the least noise made him jump. Then uncharacteristically, he snapped at Jay over something trivial. We could only stare at Don as we heard anger in his voice. Suddenly he looked frightened.

"San! What's wrong with me?" he whispered.

I made some excuse about his being tired, but neither of us believed it. Something terrible was happening deep within him.

Three days after Christmas, it was time to return to the hospital. Before we left Jay and Holly with my family, Don held them next to him for several minutes.

Back at the hospital, another round of tests was ordered as the doctors tried to figure out what to do with this patient who had beaten their medical odds. First, they decided to implant a reservoir in Don's scalp to eliminate the painful lumbar punctures. Then several hours later, they ordered a lung scan to check for possible blood clots that might be causing the sudden shortness of breath.

When the porter came to take Don to the scan room, I asked if I could please accompany him. None of the others had allowed me in the test area, but she shrugged. "Sure. Come on."

As I helped Don sit up, he gestured toward the needlepoint bag. "Might as well bring that too. These tests take forever."

In the scan room, he asked to see the Pharaoh again and then smiled sadly as I turned the *almost* completed project toward him. Oh, how I wished I'd been able to finish it long ago. Then the technician asked him to blow into a white tube so she could test his lung capacity. As I watched, I found myself puffing, too, willing him my lung capacity.

Then she asked him to lie on his stomach, holding his breath, while the scan recorded the lung profile. I watched the familiar dots outline one full lung and then begin the top of the other. But the dots stopped. Nothing showed below the top quarter of the lung! I stared at the screen. *Oh, Father, it's going to be very soon, isn't it?*

Finally the tests were complete. I stood aside as orderlies put him on the gurney. Suddenly his face went white.

"Oh, I'm so dizzy," he said.

Then he made one horrible, strangling sound, as his body arched. A technician ran for the doctor in the next room while I stood there, useless.

I couldn't watch as the doctor rushed in. All I could do was listen to those awful sounds.

Oh, Father, help! was the only prayer my pounding heart formed. Immediately I felt tangible arms around me, squeezing my shoulders. I knew no one was near me.

I heard the code blue command go out. Within seconds, green-garbed technicians burst into the room.

The doctor turned to me as they thrust the cart near Don.

"Mrs. Aldrich, please excuse us."

I nodded, willing to let them do whatever they had to. Someone guided me toward the door, past Don. I looked at him, his beautiful blue eyes wide open and staring. "Good-bye, Donnie," I whispered.

Within a few minutes, one of the doctors joined me in the waiting room. "Mrs. Aldrich, it's serious, but we're doing all we can."

I looked at him, still feeling tangible, unseen arms around me. "This is the preparation, isn't it?" I said. "First you tell me how bad it is, then you'll tell me he's gone."

How vulnerable the doctor seemed. "It *is* very bad. But we're trying to resuscitate him now."

Then he left. *Resuscitate.* They were trying to bring Don *back.*

What would he come back to? I'd seen and heard too much in that room just now. If they brought him back, he'd have to go through that all over again. *Lord, I want Don—but Your will only. Your will only.*

Then the doctor was back, accompanied by Don's oncologist. I looked at those young faces. "He's gone, isn't he?"

They nodded sadly as they sat down.

I wanted to comfort them. "You know that we both have a strong personal faith," I said, not realizing I hadn't used the past tense for Don. "I'm convinced the Lord showed mercy by taking him quickly now and sparing him worse things in the future."

The one sitting next to me gripped my arm. "And you don't know the horrible things he was spared," he said. "You hang on to that in the days ahead."

Tumbling together were my thoughts of Don's uncharacteristic personality traits and partial paralysis. In his hospital wing, I'd seen signs outside a patient's room stating "Patient is blind" but hadn't understood until that moment that Don's cancer would have destroyed the sight in those beautiful eyes. To push away the thought of Don's being blind, I asked what had caused his death.

"Pulmonary embolus" was the immediate answer. At my questioning look, they offered the translation of "massive blood clots to the lungs." I thought of the partial lung I'd seen outlined on the screen and closed my eyes.

The following days were a blur of somehow getting through them. My parents arrived at the hospital to escort me home. There, I immediately told Jay and Holly. Ten-year-old Jay searched my face, as though hoping I was telling some terrible joke. Then he threw himself against me, sobbing. Eight-year-old Holly just stared at me, her blank eyes betraying her incomprehension.

During the day, I made funeral arrangements. During the night, I stared into the shadows, remembering the sounds I'd heard when Don died. At one point, I heard someone moving cars in the driveway. I didn't bother to see who it was because I didn't care. Any strength I once might have shown had evaporated with Don's last breath.

Finally it was time to go to the funeral home. I had been dreading that first viewing, but suddenly I wanted to be near my beloved Scotsman again. I gripped Jay's and Holly's hands as together we walked toward the casket I had picked out just two days earlier.

Both children stood quietly beside me. For several minutes, I just looked at Don, remembering those long hours in the hospital when I had held his hand, watching his breath come out through his lips in little puffs. I remembered how warm and sweet his breath had been upon my face the day he reminded me the Lord never promised to give us an easy road. And I could almost hear him repeat a portion of the Twenty-third Psalm: "Yea, though I walk through the valley of the shadow of death, I will fear no evil: for thou art with me."

I patted Don's shoulder, thinking of the struggle he had waged and the grief we three would face without him.

"Ah, Donnie, you're free. You're free!" I whispered.

And from the other side of that valley, I'm sure he grinned at me.

Simple Reminders

1. "Who told you the Christian walk is supposed to be a walk? It's a slugfest!"

2. "The Lord never promised us an easy road, but He did promise to always be with us on that road."

3. Often when the very thing we dread becomes a reality, we find that it has lost some of its terror.

4. The most important thing is not material possessions but each other.

3 Understanding Grief

Different Losses, Different Pain

My life had revolved around Don, so it was—and is—only because of the Lord that I've developed a new identity. In the process, I have learned that all of us lose something precious at one time or another. And I do wish I were the last widow. But everybody hurts— even those who haven't suffered loss through death (yet) or divorce have lost in other significant ways. Prisoners grieve the loss of their freedom, those who move grieve leaving friends and familiar surroundings, adults grieve for their youth, and patients grieve over lost health.

I'm convinced that our bodies are constructed in such a way that we must grieve. And if we aren't allowed to grieve appropriately, we will express it inappropriately, often through anger or depression.

In later chapters we'll take an in-depth look at anger and depression, but first allow me to define two important terms—bereavement and grief.

Bereavement is the *time* after a major loss. The outer signs, such as wearing black or having annual memorial services—such as the Ethiopians do—are set by societies.

Grief is an *emotional response* and can stay with us for years. But a thin line exists between grieving the loss of someone we love and grieving the way our life has turned out. We all know people who display grief so intensely even years after a death that they're difficult to be around since they are convinced no one else has suffered as they have.

During the year I worked on a funeral-home counseling team with Dr. John Canine, a Detroit area grief therapist, part of my job was to encourage new widows. Of course I knew the widows' pain all too well, but while I agreed that Don's death was an amputation, I had decided it didn't always have to bleed. Most women found comfort in my soothing, "It may always hurt, but it won't always hurt *this* much."

Then one of the women brought her friend, whom I'll call Fanny, to the widows' group. Fanny sobbed throughout the introductions. Then after she told her story, I nodded comfortingly as I asked, "How long has it been?"

"Nineteen years!" was her sobbing answer.

Nineteen years? She wasn't grieving for her husband; she was dealing with unresolved issues—including guilt. Nothing I said unstuck her. She had decided long ago that she would remain miserable for the rest of her life.

GRIEF INTENSIFIERS

The grieving process may be complicated by the individual situation, but the intensity with which we grieve often depends on a combination of four variables: the closeness of the relationship and whether the death was sudden, premature, or violent. Any one of these characteristics means intense sorrow, but with each additional grief intensifier, our emotional pain deepens.

Closeness of the Relationship

This normally applies to spouses, children, siblings, or parents but can include distant relatives if a special bond was shared—such as I had with a cherished uncle.

Profound grief also occurs when a close friend dies. After Don's death, our friend Gail asked her Sunday school class to pray for me. Later a woman touched her arm and said, "And I'm praying for you, too, dear." That simple statement gave Gail permission to cry, releasing pain.

Sudden Death

How many times do we hear of the death of someone and say, "But I just saw him yesterday morning!"?

If cancer holds any redeeming factor, it's the time it gives us to think about death. This feeling, called "anticipatory grief," begins as soon as the doctor pronounces the diagnosis.

Premature Death

We tend to think of a child or young adult when we hear of "premature death." But the term can be aptly applied to those much older. We all know people who go to the doctor on Tuesday for an annual checkup and hear, "You're the healthiest seventy-seven-year-old I've ever seen." And then he drops dead on Friday. That's premature, and the widow doesn't want to hear that he had a good life. That phrase has no comfort until she can say it.

My friend Lillian was ninety-four when she received word that her ninety-six-year-old sister had died after going to Hollywood to live with her grandson. Lillian sadly commented, "I just know all that wild living shortened her life." (May *my* life be shortened at ninety-six by "wild" living!) But Lillian knew her sister was looking forward to a marvelous party on her one hundredth birthday. In that sense, her death was indeed "premature."

Violent Death

Whether it's murder, suicide, horrible accident, or war, we can't stand the thought of a loved one suffering a violent death. While I worked for an army ROTC unit during the Vietnam War, our officers were often called on to tell parents their son had been killed. The stunned silence often was broken first by the mother's question, "Did he suffer?"

Our officers usually didn't have that information, but one of them always replied, "It was quick. Very quick."

Each of these grief intensifiers carries its own pain. Of course we feel sorrow when the eighty-nine-year-old grandmother dies, but if she had been ill for a long time and died peacefully with her family around her, we come to terms with the loss fairly quickly. But our sorrow isn't always so neatly handed to us. What do we do when the sorrow comes wrapped in a close relationship or friendship and is sudden, premature, *and* violent?

During my fifteen years of high-school teaching in Garden City, Michigan, several of my students died. Seventeen-year-old Greg was murdered in a senseless robbery at the gas station where he worked. Tim was seventeen when his leg was amputated because of cancer. He died only months later. Brilliant Steve would have been in his late thirties now, but he remains in my heart as the eternal eighteen-year-old who fell four stories from his college parking ramp.

I remember the handsome fifteen-year-old in his jean jacket, grinning and saying, "Hey, I'm okay, Mrs. A" just before he went home to take the top of his head off with a shotgun blast. Rosie was fourteen when a car on Ford Road slammed into her. Vietnam took not only three of my classmates but sixteen of Garden City's students. I remember their grace on the football field or shyness in asking the girl in English class to the prom—and I hurt.

Suicide, war, murder, accident, devastating disease. Death often is absolutely senseless and even my refuge of the sovereignty of God doesn't offer a satisfactory explanation. How tired our heavenly Father must be of our blaming Him for the consequences of human decisions! I've finally settled on this: Our only choice in the midst of tragedy isn't *whether* we'll go through it but *how*. Only the Lord's presence offers comfort—and the hope that we will see our loved ones again.

BE ACTIVELY INVOLVED IN THE GRIEF PROCESS

Just as the spectators at the tomb of Lazarus (John 11) were asked to participate in the miracle of the raising of a dead man through rolling away the stone from the tomb (v. 39) and untying the graveclothes that bound the risen Lazarus (v. 44), we, too, have a responsibility to be actively involved in grief's process, as the following thoughts illustrate.

Turn Tragedy into Triumph

I truly believe that God in His re-creative way can bring His good out of our pain, but I also believe that we have to be willing to see the good that is created. But how do we accomplish that when the loss is so senseless? Granted, sometimes the victories are small by themselves, and it's only in the comparison of how we *used* to be that the miracle is seen. I'm convinced that even the most tragic loss ultimately can be turned into good—if we allow it to be. Some people start support groups to reach out to others. Some fight the things that took their child, such as the women who cofounded Mothers Against Drunk Driving (MADD) after their daughters were killed, thus saving numerous lives.

Look at Your Own Mortality

After Don's death, I was forced to look at my own mortality. Suddenly I understood my Kentucky grandmother's long-ago admonishment: "Honey, none of us were put here to stay." Somehow, I never believed that until Don was lying cold and silent against the satin pillow. If clowns can die, then we all will. That new awareness should not create panic but a new sense of the preciousness of this moment.

Make New Discoveries

The good that can come out of a tragedy doesn't have to be dramatic. Through Don's death, I've discovered I have strength I'd never recognized. And my heart is larger toward others. There's an enormous number of hurting folks out there—folks I never would have seen if it hadn't been for my own pain. And I played the "tough guy" role long enough to know that often behind the toughest, strongest exterior is the biggest hurt.

To remind me to look for the good that can still come in the midst of life's zigzags, I now have the finished needlepoint, the Pharaoh, framed and on our bedroom wall. Oh, it stayed in a drawer for five years where I had tossed it after coming home from the hospital the afternoon Don died. All that time I couldn't look at it since the memory of my failure to finish it for my dear clown was still too painful. Then on the fifth anniversary of Don's death, I answered fifteen-year-old Jay's question "Whatever happened to that needlepoint?" by hauling it out again. As I picked up the metallic thread, the last color I had needed to finish, I felt as though I'd tossed everything into the drawer just the week before. But then I realized that my eyes had deteriorated so much I had trouble threading the needle. . . . If nothing else, their weakened condition emphasized how long Don had been dead.

Today the Pharaoh is no longer a painful memory but a symbol of my life—awkward and full of mistakes, crooked stitches, and bumpy knots—but still containing beauty and strength.

Simple Reminders

1. Bereavement is the time after a major loss. Grief is the emotional response.

2. The loss through death will always be an amputation, but it does not always have to bleed.

3. The length of time that we grieve often depends on a combination of four variables: the closeness of the relationship and whether the death was sudden, premature, or violent.

4. Anticipatory grief may very well be cancer's one redeeming factor.

5. Just as the spectators at the tomb of Lazarus were asked to participate in the miracle, we, too, have a responsibility to be actively involved in grief's process.

6. God in His re-creative way can bring His good out of our pain.

4 Moving *through* the Grief
Putting One Foot in Front of the Other

At a Michigan grief seminar, a pastor interrupted my outlining of the stages of grief to bluntly ask, "How can I get my people over their grief?"

That poor man was carrying an unrealistic burden. "Your job isn't to get them *over* it," I answered. "Your job is to help them *through* it."

He visibly relaxed and settled in for the rest of my presentation in which I explained the four basic stages of grief—numbness, searching, disorientation, and resolution. I further explained that I wasn't using the stages to pigeonhole people but to help them through a confusing, frightening time. We don't move through those stages in precise order, however. Not only does grief come in waves, but it's influenced by feelings of abandonment, guilt, and emotional struggles with other family members. Often, just when we think we can handle the situation, we are reminded of our loss, and the emotional pain swells again. And we don't move from one point to another in a straight line. At times we'll move back and forth from one stage to another—especially in the latter stages.

Dr. Elisabeth Kubler-Ross found that the *dying* work through five basic stages: denial, anger, bargaining, depression, and acceptance.[1] We now know that the *families* of the terminally ill go through these stages too.

But after the death, the griever faces additional challenges through numbness, searching, disorientation, and resolution. I'm aware that some researchers have further divided these categories into nine groups, but that gets too complicated for me. I prefer the following four.

NUMBNESS

Numbness can last from just a few hours to several weeks. Everything seems to move in slow motion, causing the grievers to feel as though they are in a bad dream or walking through a fog.

As the numbness begins to fade, the intense grief of this early stage may produce chest pains or feelings of suffocation. Don had trouble breathing the morning before he died, so after his death my mind translated his suffering into my own shortness of breath. I checked with my doctor, who ran the usual medical checks then assured me that my heart and lungs were fine. I wore V-neck blouses instead of the bow ones that were popular at the time and waited for the smothering sensation to pass. Within a couple of weeks, my breathing was back to normal.

Drastic weight gains or losses can occur during the early stages of grief. Since grieving takes enormous physical strength, it isn't unusual to lose weight even without trying. When the body has worked through the initial trauma and is getting ready to rejoin life, the weight often is regained without a change in eating habits.

Massive weight gains can also occur. Often people stuff their emotions by overdosing on high calories. One woman complained that she had gained twenty pounds the first month after her husband's death. They had always taken a walk together after dinner. Now she had not only lost the motivation to take the walk, but she was trying to soothe her pain by eating childhood comfort foods of chocolate cake and cream puffs.

SEARCHING

Searching—the next stage—can be an intense time as the grievers come out of the fog and ask, "What exactly happened?" In the early part of this stage, the survivors will want to see the autopsy report or police account. Not only is it normal, but it is healthy. Getting our questions answered, painful though the process may be, gives us some emotional control.

The latter part of this stage often produces a literal searching. After Don's death, I caught myself scanning the mall crowds for him. That's even after I had seen him die. How much worse the searching must be for those who don't have their questions answered.

Questions

During the searching stage, that awful question "Why?" surfaces. Often it's accompanied by "What else could I have done?" or "Should he have stayed on the chemotherapy?" or "Maybe he should have gotten off the chemotherapy." Of course this is a painful time for those listening to the griever's questions too. No quick answers exist. After Peter Marshall's funeral, his anguished widow, Catherine, asked her mother why this had happened. Her mother, also a widow, answered quietly, "In God's time, He will give you His answers."

With hindsight we see that the Lord brought blessings out of pain as He gave Catherine her special ministry. Countless people have been comforted by writings that could not have been produced except through her own suffering.

Comparisons

The searching stage can be especially challenging for those grieving the death of a child. Suddenly the "perfect" child has died, adding an additional emotional burden to the other children: "Sharon wouldn't have left her room in such a mess." "Sharon wouldn't have slapped her brother." "Sharon wouldn't have brought home a grade like this."

Obviously, enormous repercussions ricochet throughout the family unless they understand what is happening. It's important that the children especially understand that their mother is *not* saying she wishes one of the other children had died in Sharon's place. She's merely reminding herself that Sharon was a special person with many good qualities—thus, giving credibility to her own grief.

Often grievers so need to remind themselves and others of the deceased's special qualities that they may tend to deify their spouses, ignoring irritating traits. They'll even say, "If ever a saint walked around, my sweetie was it." Or, "I'll never find anyone as good." Such statements can be tough to listen to, especially if you remember only the deceased's less-desirable qualities. For the first six months, grievers often need to concentrate on all of the good qualities, thus adding validity to their special loss. Later, they can start looking at the whole person.

The old joke says the pastor asked the rhetorical question, "Can any of us say we are perfect? If you are, stand up right now."

One man in the fifth row stood up. The pastor was astounded. "Are you perfect?"

"No, I'm not," the man replied. "I'm just standing on behalf of my wife's first husband."

Guilt

Guilt can be a major problem during the searching stage. The best way to dispel it is by expressing it. Before I worked as part of a funeral-home counseling team, I thought guilt was the plain old vanilla type that makes me visit relatives when I'm already up to my eyebrows in work. But I've since learned that three types of guilt exist: true, false, and misplaced.

True guilt. This guilt shows up when we've done something wrong and we need to say, "I'm sorry. Will you forgive me?"

But what if the person is dead, and you can't ask forgiveness? Two simple things will help: Write a letter or send a message through a prayer. Of course the letter can't be sent (although some people "mail" them by putting them into a special notebook or burning them in the fireplace), but it's therapeutic just to express all those things you wish you could say.

"I'm sorry. Please forgive me" are five of the most cleansing words in our language. Every counselor knows that having the griever express all those searing thoughts on paper or to an empty chair is an effective tactic to relieve guilt.

The same healing comes when we send a message through our prayer. A simple, heartfelt apology offers release from tormenting thoughts.

One of my friends, whom I'll call Joy, tells how stricken she was when a recent widower in her church died. Just a few weeks earlier she'd requested that he postpone his frequent calls until later in the evening: He had called several times just as she was preparing dinner for her family. He never called again.

In the rush of her schedule, Joy forgot about him—until he died. At the funeral home, his out-of-state daughter greeted her with a hug, saying that he had commented about how much it helped him to talk to Joy.

"After Mother died, the dinner hour was awful for him since he and Mother used to cook together and catch up on the day's news," the daughter said. "You helped him so much. Thank you."

The next several days were rough for Joy as she replayed those phone calls and her request that they stop. She gave herself pep talks emphasizing how busy her large family kept her and how rude he had been to call during her busiest time of the day. The guilt remained.

Finally one evening, she knelt by her bed and said through her tears, "Lord, please tell him I'm sorry. I didn't realize what those calls meant to him."

Peace finally arrived—along with a new sensitivity to the grieving people around her.

False guilt. This guilt—and the next—are two of Satan's favorite tools to torment the griever. False guilt is exactly that—false. It's expressed most often through phrases such as "I should have." "I should have insisted he have the surgery." Or "I should have insisted he not have the surgery."

Several years ago, dear neighbors were involved in an automobile accident just before Christmas. Everyone survived, but the eight-year-old daughter had to have extensive operations on her foot. Two days after the accident, I drove the father to the nearby town where his insurance adjuster had totaled out the van. On the way there, he kept saying, "It's all my fault. We should have stayed home."

He needed more than a listener. "Look," I said, "this was an annual family dinner that you've always attended. What if you'd stayed home and she'd gotten hurt? Wouldn't you be saying, 'We should have gone'? What you're feeling right now is so common that counselors even have a name for it—false guilt. *You* didn't cut her foot. That happened when the van hit a patch of ice."

Relief swept over his face. Then we could talk about the distortion guilt brings to any situation, especially to the parent who feels he must protect his family from all of life's hurts.

My neighbor was able to verbalize his pain to someone who could help put it in the proper perspective. But if it isn't acknowledged, it grows. Another friend was involved in an accident that resulted in her father's death. Her own injuries kept her from attending his funeral but not from dwelling on the tragedy. A year later, she sobbed to me, "I killed my papa."

In her family's culture, life's traumas weren't discussed, they were merely borne. But this hurt was too great for her to carry alone. For more than an hour, I talked about the various types of guilt, stressing that she hadn't killed her father, the accident had. But even reminders that he wouldn't want her punishing herself made no difference as she kept saying, "No, I killed him."

Nothing I said stopped her sobs. Finally I asked her to pray in her language for God's help and to send a message to her father. For several moments, she prayed as tears ran down her cheeks. I couldn't understand the words but I understood the emotion, and a definite peace settled over her near the end of her prayer. When she looked up, I took her hands into mine.

"How did your father die?" I asked.

She looked at me, bewildered. Hadn't she been explaining his death to me for the last hour? But suddenly recognition flooded her face, and she answered, "He died in an auto accident," instead of "I killed him." She had taken the first step toward healing.

Misplaced guilt. Guilt of this nature occurs when a normal situation explodes out of proportion. Years ago, before Easter corsages were sold in the local variety stores, Carl always ordered a corsage from the florist for his wife. But one Easter they had been so busy with parenting a new baby and purchasing their first home that he forgot—until Easter morning. Slapping his forehead in frustration, he apologized repeatedly. His wife had laughed and heartily hugged him, saying she already had everything that she wanted and that flowers didn't matter. Two weeks later, when she was killed in an automobile accident, it mattered very much. The forgotten flowers tormented Carl, and no amount of bouquets at the funeral could make up for that unpurchased corsage.

DISORIENTATION

Disorientation can be scary because, while we come to grips with the idea we must go on with our lives, the only way we can hang on to the one we lost is by looking backward. Trying to move in two directions at once can result in great emotional distress.

Old Possessions

During the disorientation stage, closets are cleaned out, clothes given to the Salvation Army, and tools and golf clubs presented to sons or best friends. To do that before the griever is ready can complicate the letting-go process. Three days after Don's funeral, his dad tried to convince me to clean out the closets before he returned to Florida. I had never before argued with him, but that day I quietly refused.

"I'm not ready to do that yet," I said.

He countered with, "You have to get rid of those things that remind you of him."

I dug my heels in. "If I do that, I'll have to get rid of everything—including the antique clock we bought on vacation, the silly coffee mugs we found at a garage sale, and even Jay and Holly! No. When I'm ready, I'll sort through his things. And not until then."

And not giving in was exactly the best thing I could have done for myself. Not only did I gain some control over my immediate future, but I also dared to tell someone what I needed. Of course it hurt to see Don's clothes hanging next to mine every morning when I opened the closet, but it also helped me adjust gradually to the fact that he wasn't coming back. I finally gave away his clothing in

March—three months later—and only when I was ready. During the sorting, I asked Jay and Holly if there were special items they wanted me to keep for them. They both chose several sports jerseys to wear with jeans. I also put aside Don's varsity jacket with his tennis letter. The spring that Jay turned fifteen, he discovered it and tried it on. It fit perfectly. He wore it for the rest of the semester and enjoyed show-ing off his vintage treasure to his school buddies.

Personal Items

When the survivors are ready to let go of the deceased's personal items, they often wonder which ones they should discard and which ones they should keep. Many counselors divide the items into two categories: *linking objects* and *mementos*.

Linking objects are personal items, such as toothbrushes, and should be discarded as quickly as the griever is comfortable with throwing them away. For years, our green ceramic toothbrush holder in the main bath held four brushes. After Don's death, the empty hole bothered me more than if I'd left his toothbrush there, so I added a different colored one for my evening brushing. Another widow solved that same dilemma by adding a toothbrush for her granddaughter's visits.

Sometimes the linking objects are a bit more bizarre. At one of my seminars, a woman asked about her sister's insistence upon sleeping on her husband's pillow because it still had his body scent on it. I assured her that in time the scent would fade and common sense and hygiene would force her to wash the material. But until then, it was normal for her to want to hang on to that smell just a bit longer.

Mementos include family pictures and heirlooms that are an important part of the family's memories. Mementos should be kept.

The family portrait that we had taken just two months before Don's death is still hanging in our upstairs hallway and still makes me smile as I pass it.

On the other hand, some mementos may cause more pain than joy. Don had won a number of golf and tennis trophies, which I dusted for two years after his death. When I finally decided I needed the shelf space for books, I asked a friend to help me clean the family room that day. Painful though it was, it was time to pack away both the object and the memory.

New Realizations

As my grief progressed through the disorientation stage, I began to remember Don as a total person, including his intense competitiveness, even when playing a simple board game, and his insistence upon handling all family finances. Not everyone was comfortable with my insight though. When a new friend asked me to describe Don, I mentioned his booming laugh, his love for others, his delight in filling our home with company. Then I added, "But he wasn't a saint."

My friend, not realizing the emotional step that admission represented for me, was horrified. "How can you say that about your husband? Don't you have any respect for his memory?"

I let her complain, secure in my new confidence.

A normal statement made during the disorientation stage is, "I'll never marry again." At the time the widow says it, she really means it. That's part of her need to deify the one she's lost, thereby reminding herself that he was so special she can never have that kind of love again.

And she won't. Even if she remarries the following year, the circumstances are different—families may be combined, careers may be changed—and life's realities have replaced her wide-eyed glow. But sooner or later, trying to remain married to a dead spouse doesn't work.

It has now been more than sixteen years since Don's death, but it took me eleven years before I would venture out even for coffee—and then only with someone I had known since the fourth grade. Not only was I too chicken-hearted to jump back into the sweaty-palms stage of meeting potential dates, but I hadn't seen enough happy second marriages to make me want to add a husband to my already hectic life. Even now, I remind myself that as long as I remain unmarried, I have the privilege of submitting only to the Lord. Yes, you may remind me of that when you hear I've nailed my navy blue suit jacket to my office door and run away with a banjo-playing gypsy.

But even as I'm arguing with myself, I remember a startling realization eighteen months after Don died. Jay, Holly, my parents, and I attended the Gun and Musket Show at Greenfield Village in Dearborn, Michigan and enjoyed historical reenactments by folks dressed to match the time period of their firearms.

As we ambled across the village green toward the Civil War recruitment tent, a ruggedly handsome Old West Cavalry officer strode toward us. From his black hat to his polished black boots, he personified masculinity. I was so taken by the sight, I breathed, "Oh, my!" without thinking. Apparently, he could read lips—or eyes—because he smiled in that slow, knowing way I hadn't seen since college and veered toward me.

Immediately I averted my eyes and scurried to catch up with my family. As I did so, a new sadness and a new awareness wrapped itself around me: My husband was dead, but I wasn't.

In the following weeks, that realization made me withdraw even more from my friends as I sorted through thoughts about my future, including a recent contact by a former boyfriend. But once I decided that I didn't want to remarry, I was free to rebuild my life, following only the Lord's direction. I was also free from the temptation to walk into a gathering and glance around, wondering who was there.

RESOLUTION

Resolution signals the beginning of rejoining life. Joy, and even laughter, returns. I felt guilty the first time I laughed after Don died even though a relative was telling a zany story about a cousin. How could I laugh when Don was lying in Oak Grove Cemetery?

In the days that followed, I pondered the lack of laughter in my life. Throughout our marriage, my humor rarely emerged because life was serious stuff. I even occasionally accused Don of not taking things seriously enough. Still, he taught me how to laugh not only at life's quirks but even at myself.

After he died, I decided I could never laugh again without the example of his booming laugh. But then as I moved through my grief, I noticed the preciousness of each moment. Don's laughter had drawn people to him, including Jay and Holly.

Even with my decision to allow laughter into my life again, my reentry into the world came gradually. Those who didn't know me during my intense stage can't believe laughter was ever foreign to me. When anything strikes me as funny now, my laughter bounces off the walls. How soon laughter or even quiet grins return to our lives depends on how intense the circumstances were that caused our grief.

But a time comes when we must allow the laughter to return—or pull our gloom even tighter around our shoulders.

Medically, laughter causes the brain to release chemicals called endorphins, which relieve pain. The late Norman Cousins used this concept in battling a rare connective tissue disease by watching comedies and reading humorous writings. He surprised the doctors by living several years beyond their expectations. When Proverbs 17:22 says "A merry heart doeth good like a medicine" (KJV), it's true!

Count the Blessings

But even as far as I've been brought by the Lord since Don's death, special occasions—such as graduations and weddings—bring fresh pain. No one moves from despair to emotional recovery in a straight line, no matter what level of grief we're dealing with. Grief comes in waves. And just about the time we take a deep breath and say, "Okay, I can do this," we get hit again.

The spring following Don's death, I thought I had survived the roughest milestones. Then one Saturday, Jay and Holly were helping me clean out the garage. On the bottom shelf we found their dad's old, ratty golf shoes I'd demanded he throw away the previous year. He had stood in the sunshine on a long-ago Saturday morning and grinned in his little-boy way that let me know he'd do whatever *he* wanted with them.

And there I was months later, holding the shoes without Don and without the sunshine and crying both at the memory and the knowledge I'd never again hear his "Ah, San." But even through my tears, I knew I had been blessed by the love of a good man, and that memory would help me over many of the rough spots.

Living Renewed

Resolution also comes when the griever says to himself, "Life goes on." One of our neighbors had taught with Don for sixteen years, so he often stopped over with reports of the school's continuing activity. Then before he'd leave, he'd add that I had to get on with my life too. More than once I thought, *If he says, "Life goes on" one more time today, I'll smack him.* Life *does* go on, but I needed to wade through all of the emotions until I could say it to myself.

During resolution a creative surge often appears. Not only does the survivor begin or intensify journal entries, but she will often look for ways to bring good out of her suffering. Some grieving parents start support groups, actively reaching out to other parents after a tragedy.

Some find peace in volunteer work. When Don was in the hospital that final time, one of the most helpful volunteers was a widow who remembered her own long days of sitting by a hospital bed during the holidays. She anticipated my needs and outlined the schedule of several of the medical departments, including when lab work was typically done.

Now that Jay and Holly are grown, I'm checking into the possibility of working in an understaffed ward during the holidays too. But even before I came to this point in my life, I sensed a new awareness of *this moment's joy* as I learned to see God's hand in the world around me. Even now as I take a walk on a beautiful summer day, I count the various shades of green. My record is fourteen.

The intense person I used to be couldn't see beauty as long as carpets lay unvacuumed and articles remained untyped. But the person I am now has learned how fragile life is and looks for healing in enjoying the wonderful things around me. If something is funny, I laugh. If the sunset is incredible, I comment on it.

Oh, I still have my moments of wanting to roll back the years to before Don's first cancer, but I'm enough of a realist to accept the loss of our position as the Perfect Family. Those days can't be called back. I can only grow from those experiences and occasionally help others cope with the losses heading their way.

Spiritual Ponderings

One thing affecting the resolution stage is how soon the survivor is able to grasp the reality of the death. Having seen Don die moved me faster toward resolution than a wife whose husband was killed in war and buried overseas. Having an object—a body, a casket, or a grave—helps us focus our grief and recognize the finality of our loss.

But that level often doesn't come without struggle over just how deeply God is involved in each life. I often remind myself, and others, that God never says, "Oops!" But does that mean He *planned* from the beginning of our marriage (in fact, from the beginning of our lives) that Don was to die at thirty-nine? Is He like some author who knows the story isn't interesting unless danger lurks, so He occasionally kills children or young parents? Or does He merely *know* the troubles that will descend upon our lives and wait for us to surrender the trauma, and ourselves, to Him so He can bring His good out of them?

As I struggled with this area, I found that I best understood the will of God when I pictured a house. Jesus stands at the front door, inviting us in. We can enter through the open door, climb in through the window, drop down the chimney, or maybe—as I have often done—first chop a few holes in the roof. We can even refuse to enter the house at all, if we mistakenly believe grief is to be our permanent fate and thereby deny ourselves His healing touch. But it is only when we offer ourselves back to the One who gave Himself for us that we finally find peace—and the determination to go on with our lives, stronger and ready to help others through their eventual suffering.

Simple Reminders

1. The four basic stages of grief—numbness, searching, disorientation, and resolution—are not to pigeonhole people but to help them understand the dynamics they are experiencing.

2. Sooner or later, trying to remain married to a dead spouse doesn't work.

3. For the first several months after a death, grievers often need to concentrate on all of the good qualities of the deceased.

4. Guilt often comes in three "flavors"—true, false, and misplaced.

5. Realizing that your spouse is dead—but you are not—can be disconcerting.

6. While it's important to face the pain of our grief, the time comes when we must allow laughter to return.

5 *Surviving the Loss*

Acknowledging the Hurt

For the first two months after Don died, I couldn't stand to be downstairs in the family room alone after Jay and Holly went to bed. So I'd go upstairs when they did, but I'd take a stack of books with me. I read everything I could find about grief, hoping to find something to help me. It took me awhile to learn that as much as I wanted to be rescued from the smothering feelings of panic, I still had choices that could help me turn toward healing.

FACE THE LOSS

It's okay to hurt. You aren't damaging your Christian testimony if you cry. It's okay to miss someone you love. Remember, even Jesus wept—over Jerusalem (Luke 19:41) and at the tomb of Lazarus (John 11:35).

Scholars have pondered the reasons why Jesus wept at the tomb of His friend Lazarus. Was He weeping out of sorrow? Out of compassion for the sisters? Out of despair at their lack of faith? I think part of the reason He was weeping was because He knew Lazarus would have to go through death again. There isn't some two-thousand-year-old guy named Lazarus wandering around Jerusalem today. Lazarus had to die again since we have not been promised eternal *earthly* life.

So if Jesus, the Son of God, can cry, it's okay for me—a frail, imperfect human—to cry.

In facing the grief, it helps to remember that some of the dumbest things are going to get to you. That realization for me came just a few days after the funeral: For almost seventeen years, Don and I shared the bathroom towel rack. One hand towel hung in the middle with our separate washcloths on either side. A couple of days after the funeral, I was putting fresh towels up. Just as I started to put the two washcloths on either side of the hand towel, it hit me that I didn't need two washcloths on the rack. Don wasn't coming back.

Talking through even those "dumb" symbols of loss with a trusted friend or a knowledgeable grief counselor can be an important step in acknowledging the hurt. Those who try to ignore looking at their distress—whether because it's too painful or because they think "good" Christians don't cry—often battle stress and depression later.

RECOGNIZE THAT PAIN COMES WITH THE TERRITORY

Something healthy happens when we say, "This hurts!" Releasing that pain may be as dramatic as sobbing on the kitchen floor, as intense as crying all evening after the children are in bed, or as quiet as a deep sigh when a young family reminds us of what we've lost.

Southerners have an expression to describe the intangible longing that occasionally sweeps over us: "feeling homesick and lonesome." The only immediate cure I've found for that pain is the Bible. Every human emotion is recorded there. Immediately Psalm 74:1 comes to mind: "Why hast thou cast us off for ever?" (KJV). Once we've accepted the reality of our situation, we can begin to work through it with the Lord's help.

ACCEPT THE UNIVERSALITY OF SUFFERING

I'm not the first widow nor will I be the last. Once the Don Aldrich family was the Perfect Family. By the world's standards, we had it all, and I thought we would have those glory days forever. Now I know all too well that everyone is going to suffer at one time or another.

I remember a Confederate soldier's letter that said in part, "Some of us are rich and some are poor. Some are old and some are young. But we all bleed the same."

The universality of suffering, no matter the culture, was illustrated in another way the Christmas following Don's death. All of us have our pet peeves. One of mine happens to be grave blankets. What are they keeping warm anyway? But Don had always liked them, saying they were a symbol that the person under them had been loved. So, of course, I bought the evergreen cover and anchored it on top of the frozen soil a few days after his funeral. With tears running down my cheeks, I whispered, "You were truly loved, Donnie."

The next year, I made my purchase as soon as the evergreens were displayed at the local florist shop. But even as I paid for it, I complained about the pagan practice of grave blankets. The Greek owner listened politely to my complaints and then asked, "What if you had to wash the bones of your husband?"

"What?"

He nodded. "On my island in Greece only the wealthy own the graves of their family. The rest of us must rent the ground for three years. At the end of that time, we dig up our dead, wash the bones, put them in a small box and place them into the burying wall. I did that for both of my parents. Grave blankets aren't such a bad custom."

I emphatically agreed.

RECOGNIZE THE POWER OF GUILT

One favorite story of every grief counselor is of two men whose mothers died in the same hospital. As the chaplain talked to them separately, the first son blamed himself for not having sent his mother to Florida.

"It's all my fault Mom died," he said. "She stayed here in this cold weather when she needed sunshine. Her death is my fault."

Later, the chaplain talked to the second man. "It's all my fault my mother died," he said. "I sent her to Florida and the change in temperature had just been too much for her system. I should have kept her here."

For those still hounding themselves with the "should-haves," they're dealing with false guilt—the kind the Enemy loves to use against us. One way to release it is to say aloud, "This is false guilt, and it is not from God." As you keep talking to God about it, the peace will eventually come.

IT'S OKAY TO TREAT YOURSELF KINDLY

One of the most common expressions of false guilt is the feeling the griever has that she shouldn't be good to herself. After all, her husband is dead: How can she buy a new dress or go out to dinner? But that's just it—we aren't dead, our husbands are. And taking care of ourselves is one of the best ways to work through the swarming guilts. That means it's okay to take a morning walk and okay to buy a new dress.

This was a difficult area for me because my whole childhood training had been in how to take care of others—a husband, babies, relatives. A few years ago, the martyr-mother jokes were popular: "Don't worry about me, dear. You go to Florida. I'll be fine. I'm happy to sit here in the dark—all by myself." Believe me, most of us can match those antics anytime. So how do we break away from it? By giving ourselves little verbal pep talks beginning with "I took good care of my husband; now it's time to take good care of myself."

GUARD YOUR HEALTH

This is a warning I didn't heed. I went from long months of fighting cancer by Don's side to facing daily challenges—and the future— alone. Not only was I worn out, but even at thirty-seven, youth was no longer on my side. And in the midst of my grief, I was still trying to help some of my relatives. I wish I'd said a few more times, "I'm sorry but I can't deal with that situation just yet" or "I can't solve that problem for you; I'm still hurting."

I offer that advice hesitantly because I don't want grievers suddenly turning into self-centered whiners. But sometimes the best way we can feel good about ourselves is by not giving in to another's unreasonable request. It's okay to go to bed earlier than ever before—

especially during the first few months. Grieving takes enormous energy, so your body needs more rest. We aren't *super* beings; we are *human* beings.

FIND THE SILVER LINING

Believe it or not, we do have the choice of whether we want to be better or bitter because of what we've experienced. What if we stopped asking "Why me?" and pondered "Why *not* me?" Why do we think we're supposed to get through this life without sorrow? Think of Job's observation: "Shall we accept good from God, and not trouble?" (Job 2:10).

Allow that grief to help you become a better person as you learn from it and help others through their pain. We can also help ourselves as we grasp the importance of *this* moment and *this* day.

Whenever I think about the importance of attitude, I'm reminded of an old rabbinical story of nine men who were living in one room and not getting along very well. They called for the rabbi to settle their problem. He looked at their sorrowful faces and said, "I can solve your problem, but you must promise to do whatever I say. Agreed?"

The men glanced at each other and reluctantly nodded. The rabbi continued. "What you must do is get a goat to live here with you for one month. The problem will be solved after those thirty days."

Adding another creature to already crowded conditions wasn't the solution the men wanted, but they had promised. Several weeks later, the rabbi saw one of the men on the street.

"Well, how are things with all of you now?" he asked.

The man beamed. "Oh, we're getting along great—now that we've gotten rid of the goat."

Their original situation had not changed, but their attitude had. And sometimes our response to our situation determines how we will cope.

KEEP A JOURNAL

My friends Carl and Marilyn Amann, both of whose first spouses had died in accidents, took down our Christmas tree the day Don died, helping me clear the house for the arrival of out-of-town relatives. As they hugged me good-night and promised to be back the next day, Carl insisted I verbalize my pain on paper. The first entry was scribbled: "How could my world have changed so suddenly in just these few hours? Don died this afternoon. Died? He can't be dead. He's my best friend, my whole world."

Later I would have only enough strength to copy Jeremiah 10:19—"Woe is me for my hurt! my wound is grievous: but I said, Truly this is a grief, and I must bear it" (KJV).

I remember one widow who wrote letters to her husband every day—just as she had when he was away on business trips. She wasn't denying his death, and she knew the letters were going into her notebook rather than into the mailbox. But every night she wrote about what she and the children had done that day, told the neighborhood gossip, or expressed frustration at the latest home- and car-maintenance problems. The routine provided a safety zone until she could face the future without him.

IT'S OKAY TO SET GOALS

Setting goals is a tough area for most of us who grieve. After all, an important part of our very being was buried along with the person we loved. But life is *not* over for us. What do you want to be doing two years from now? Still sitting in the orange chair, watching TV? Volunteering at the hospital? Working with teen drug addicts? Whatever goals we have for the future have their roots in the decisions we make today.

After Margo got over the initial pain of her son's death caused by a drunk driver, she answered her own questions about the future by completing her degree and teaching high school. For the next eighteen years, she had a direct influence upon several hundred teens a year and was instrumental in establishing drinking awareness programs.

•

ACCEPT THE CHANGES

For the first several weeks after Don's death I refused to serve dinner at the family table. I simply couldn't face that fourth—empty—chair. Instead, we three hit the fast-food places or ate in the family room while we watched reruns of *M*A*S*H*.

Finally I decided I'd dodged the issue long enough. So for supper that evening, we sat at the table and, out of habit, put our hands toward each other for the blessing on the food. But the round table was too large, and our hands didn't reach. We needed Don there to fill that hole. I covered my face with my hands and sobbed.

The next evening, I faced the dinner hour with the same dread. But the three of us needed structure if we were going to retain our status as a family, so I invited Jay and Holly back to the table, saying, "I won't cry this time." I also sat in Don's chair—so we wouldn't have to look at its emptiness—and we didn't try to hold hands across the large table as we prayed. Gradually we became comfortable again in that setting.

The holidays took major changes. Don's favorite holiday meal was the traditional Thanksgiving dinner. But after he died, I couldn't cook if he wasn't there to say, "Great meal, San."

However, for the sake of my children, I couldn't spend the day in bed either. Several of our friends had invited us for dinner, but I didn't want to spend the day with someone else's Perfect Family. If I was going to compare myself to others, I wanted the comparison going in the right direction.

So I called the Salvation Army and offered myself, eleven-year-old Jay, and ten-year-old Holly to help serve dinner. That was exactly the right decision. Two minutes of watching single mothers, street people, the elderly, and even intact families come in for a holiday meal showed me another world.

The closest I came to tears that day was when the captain led us in a chorus before the dinner. The contrast of my previous Thanksgiving when I had cooked for Don and the relatives was just too much; I wanted to sob.

But I blinked back the tears as I looked at the others in the hall. What had they lost? What about the smiling woman with the white summer-weight dress? Had she once cooked for a large family? Perhaps her husband had given her shoulders a tight squeeze and whispered, "Great meal, Hon."

Or how about that polite man in the shabby suit? Did he live in one of the downtown hotels, and had he come for the company as well as the food? Gradually I set aside my own problems. I had discovered the difference between being miserable and acting miserably.

Another major change I made was giving myself permission to travel—especially in the summer. Don hadn't wanted to leave our summer place on the shore of Lake Michigan, and for us to have separate vacations was unthinkable. The first summer after his death, Jay, Holly, and I drove to Kentucky to visit relatives I hadn't seen in years.

Of course not all the changes we make have to be that dramatic. Even something as simple as changing the bathroom colors from brown to peach can be satisfying. Or wearing purple instead of the pink he always purchased for you.

But the best changes are the ones we make in ourselves. Ephesians 4:31–32 says, "Get rid of all bitterness, rage and anger, brawling and slander, along with every form of malice. Be kind and compassionate to one another, forgiving each other, just as in Christ God forgave you." The best results come from our determination to change our attitudes toward life and others.

LEARN TO FORGIVE

My friend Karen had trouble forgiving herself for "letting" her husband die. Even though her extended care of him had damaged her health, she was tormented by the thought she could have done more. One evening, as she prayed, she cried aloud, "What *didn't* I do?"

Within her spirit, she heard the gentle reply: *You did all you could.* As future self-accusations came, she recalled that thought and gradually learned to let go of the rest.

Forgiving others, though, was even more tricky—especially as she thought of her husband's own father who ignored countless opportunities to encourage him. But she knew John 13:34–35 wasn't to be trifled with: "A new command I give you: Love one another. As I have loved you, so you must love one another. By this all men will know that you are my disciples, if you love one another."

Mark 11:25 was just as relentless: "And when you stand praying, if you hold anything against anyone, forgive him, so that your Father in heaven may forgive you your sins."

Again, prayer was Karen's only refuge as she worked through complicated emotions. Like a scared, angry little kid, she listed years of accumulated gripes. And she had no safer place to dump all her misery than in the Lord's lap. Aren't you glad that when he said "Come unto me" (Matthew 11:28 KJV), He didn't add "But make sure your attitude is right first"?

So, determined to be a good spiritual example for her children, Karen set her jaw and continued sending notes to her father-in-law, extending the usual invitations for dinner. Gradually, she noticed that it became absolutely delicious to return "good for evil." Then the most amazing thing happened: Her relationship with those relatives became genuine. As she supplied the right action—and continued to pray— the sincere attitude followed until she was able to forgive others even without their having asked. She felt no dramatics. Just peace.

Simple Reminders

1. You aren't damaging your Christian testimony if you cry. Even Jesus wept.

2. It's not only okay to treat yourself kindly during bereavement, it's absolutely essential.

3. When Jesus said "Come unto me," He did not add "But come without tears."

4. We have the choice of allowing grief to make us better or bitter.

5. As you supply the right action toward those who have hurt you, the right emotion will eventually come.

6 How to Help Others
Listening May Be Your Greatest Encouragement

Perhaps you aren't the one grieving but want to help someone who is. The tendency, of course, is to do nothing. After all, you don't want to remind others of their grief. Believe me, every breath is a reminder that life will never again be the same. So, go ahead and remind those who are grieving—of your concern, special memories, and even helplessness. Your comments may very well be that day's (or week's!) blessing. Here are several things you can do to help your friend grieve appropriately:

ENCOURAGE THE GRIEVER TO TALK

People who care about others want to say something that will ease the pain, but it's more important to hurt with them.

The most important thing you can do is listen. Listen while the mother describes the squealing brakes and the sight of her six-year-old lying facedown in the street. The easy thing is to say, "No, that's okay. I don't need the details." But she needs to give them, painful though they are.

IDENTIFY THE SOURCE OF PAIN

As a friend listens to the griever, he often hears what the person is really saying. The two most common emotions are anger and guilt—and they're often tangled together.

One grief counselor listened to a widow rant against the hospital for sending her husband home when his tumor wasn't responding to chemotherapy.

"They should have kept him there," she said. "He was too sick to be home. He was so confused he couldn't find the bathroom and went in our bedroom instead. Those stupid doctors!"

As the counselor asked questions, he learned the man had died a few days after the incident. The woman was actually angry at herself for having yelled at her confused husband. When he identified the source of her anger, she sobbed. Once she faced the anger, she could allow the healing to begin.

HELP SORT OUT FEELINGS

We feel better when we can express our feelings. If it's a glorious morning, somehow verbalizing that thought makes the day even better. And if we can verbalize the painful feelings, the pain is lessened. This is where a good listener can make a big difference. Without sounding clinical, we can say, "How are you doing—really? Feel like talking?"

In our society denial and avoidance are two common reactions to loss. Denial is the "This isn't happening to me" feeling. Avoidance is the "Okay, it happened. Now I'm going to forget about it." Both can cause later problems. Identifying the emotion can open the way to the needed release and healing.

Often anger seeps through the words. Perhaps it's directed toward the rotten weather that made the roads slippery that day, the police-man who responded to the call, God for letting the person die, or even the deceased himself. All that is normal. The griever needs to hear that it's okay to be angry, even at the deceased or at God. Notice that I didn't say "desirable," but "okay."

Many people are uncomfortable with the thought that it's okay to be angry at God. They mouth all the right words about God's comfort, but deep down they wonder: *If He's so good, how come He didn't stop the tragedy?* I decided long ago that God can handle our anger. He knows our hearts and sees the anger anyway, so why shouldn't we talk to Him about it?

God is so real to me that I dare to gripe at Him when my life is turned inside out. Oh, I want to be one of those placid saints who never complains and immediately accepts everything as coming from His hand and is, therefore, wonderful. But even with my strong faith, I have a long way to go before I can watch a young life dissolve before my eyes and then say, "Hey, that's neat, God. Thanks!" But I have seen Him bring His good out of whatever we give to Him. And He will comfort us in tangible and profound ways—if we'll let Him.

The anger that's part of every grief can be constructive or destructive. Constructive anger forms support groups—such as

Friends and Families, a group for those who have lost loved ones through murder—or educational groups such as Mothers against Drunk Driving. Destructive anger lashes out at everyone around it or turns inward in the form of depression or illness. It's not uncommon for that anger to be misdirected toward others.

When I gave grief presentations before doctors' groups, I could always get their attention by remarking that patients' survivors who have unresolved anger are more apt to file malpractice suits. They were ready to listen then.

Unexpressed anger can be detrimental too. For example, a friend I'll call Becky tells about her then nine-year-old son, Johnny, screaming as he charged into the house. With his left hand, he was clutching the right, and blood was oozing from between his fingers.

"Johnny! What happened? Let me see!"

"No! You'll hurt me!"

"Honey, I can't help unless you show me your hand."

"No! Get away!"

Finally Becky had to wrestle him down to see the injury. As she carefully opened his fingers, she expected to see tendon and bone, but it was only one of those top-layer-off scrapes that bleed a lot. After washing and dressing the wound, Becky released Johnny to return to his ball game.

As she put away the first-aid kit, she marveled at Johnny's refusal to let her help. Suddenly Becky was struck with the thought that she'd been doing the same thing to God. Her ex-husband's abandonment had so hurt her she couldn't even pray about it. It was as though God was saying, "Let me see your hurt," while Becky had stood with fists clenched as she inwardly shouted, "No! You'll hurt me even more!"

Don't Condemn Emotions

Romans 12:15 is the perfect verse for those who want to help the griever: "Rejoice with those who rejoice; mourn with those who mourn." It's important that the griever have freedom to express the needed emotions—tears, of course, but even laughter. It's unfortunate when others think everyone should grieve at the same pace. Thus, if those judgmental people see the widow laughing, they think, *Boy, it certainly didn't take her long to get over him.* Believe me, she's not over her grief; she's merely enjoying the momentary joke.

Those first weeks back at our summer place after Don's death were made easier by special friends who supported rather than judged my moods. Often when I cried, they cried with me. And if I needed to laugh, they rejoiced. Their acceptance of whatever emotion I displayed helped move me that much closer to healing.

The first Sunday after the funeral can be terribly difficult for many people, especially if they were together in church the previous week. In one short week, the person has died, the funeral has taken place, and everything has changed. My first Sunday back, I walked Jay and Holly to their classes, then I entered the large sanctuary all by myself.

As Dr. Hess preached, I missed Don's nudges. Then I missed hearing his tenor voice reaching the high notes during the closing hymn. But I was there every Sunday and listened with tears running down my cheeks. Finally, one early September morning, eight and a half months after Don's death, I knew my healing had finally begun when, at the end of the sermon, I smiled at Dr. Hess.

Once I apologized to him for crying every Sunday. His reply was gentle. "You aren't alone. The important thing is you kept coming, kept being open to the message and what God had for you."

I'm grateful that God understands our pain and will help us through our grief. I'm also thankful that He doesn't expect our smiles of acceptance to come right away.

Shortly before we moved to New York, one of the women at church said to me, "Oh, you had the most marvelous testimony after Don. You never cried; you were just a pillar of strength."

I was first astounded, then irritated. "No, you just never saw me cry. I'm sorry if that weakens my testimony, but remember, even Jesus cried."

Undoubtedly, I disappointed her, but someday she, too, will lose someone she loves. If I had lied to her, allowing her to believe that "good" Christians don't cry even in the worst sorrow, then I would have been doing her a disservice by heaping guilt upon her future tears. Or worse yet, perhaps she wouldn't have given herself permission to cry and would have locked all of that pain inside. We are truly "fearfully and wonderfully made" (Psalm 139:14). God knew what He was doing when He gave us tear ducts. In fact, when we're under stress, crying is a healthy thing for us to do. In the early eighties, William H. Frey II, Ph.D., the director of the Alzheimer's Research Laboratories at Ramsey Medical Center in St. Paul, Minnesota, led a team of researchers testing the content of tears. By comparing the tears shed when the subjects peeled onions against the tears shed when those same people watched a sad movie, the researchers discovered noticeable chemical differences.[1]

But haven't we always known that? Think of the times we've responded to "What's wrong?" with "Nothing. I just need a good cry."

If we're not allowed to cry because of our own or society's standards, I'm convinced the brain holds the toxins that should be released, thus producing other problems. It's better if the tears can flow now so we can move on later. That's why the friends who were the greatest comfort to me were the ones who simply put their arms around me and cried too.

AVOID HOOF-IN-MOUTH COMFORTING

No one quoting Romans 8:28 comforted me. In fact, I felt as though they had come to do their good Christian duty before going out to dinner. When they walked out the door, they may have felt better, but I certainly didn't.

Let me stress that I do believe Romans 8:28: "And we know that in all things God works for the good of those who love him, who have been called according to his purpose." But I need to get to the place where I can quote it to myself—and believe it—rather than hear it quoted by someone else.

Know what amazed me though? The women who said they knew just how I felt as they stood there with their husbands! But the prize for the worst "comfort" comes from a letter to Ann Landers several years ago: A friend visited the parents of a nine-year-old son who had been tragically killed. "I know just how you feel," she said. "Our dog died a month ago, and we're still grieving." Remember, Job's friends sat with him for seven days and never got into trouble until they opened their mouths.

HONOR THOSE PROMISES

Another way to help someone move through grief is by fulfilling promises. A favorite parting at the funeral home is "Call me if you need anything." But two months pass, and everyone has gotten on with life—except the griever. Suddenly the widow realizes her car needs tires, but she doesn't know where to get new ones. She will be able to move back into life faster if she gets help from the first person she calls. Being put off or hearing too soon, "You've got to learn to make these decisions yourself" turns her away from grieving for an individual and into grieving for the way her life has changed.

OFFER PRACTICAL HELP

I'll never forget answering the door the day after Don's funeral and finding my friend Nancy Harrison there. Timidly she said, "I've come to help you clean your house, if you'll let me. I didn't call because I knew you'd say you were fine."

Not only did Nancy offer to meet a *specific* need, but she stepped through my emotional wall and risked rejection in order to help. I wisely let her in, and we worked together all morning organizing the chaos I had ignored during Don's last hospital stay. The best thing that happened that morning was the further deepening of our friendship.

I advise caution here, though, because not everyone has the same needs. For example, a widower may need help in normal household tasks if his wife handled the laundry, grocery shopping, and cooking. Others may have been the principal cooks for years but are suddenly bewildered by the checkbook. The most important thing we can do is ask in what areas they need help.

SAME PAIN, DIFFERENT RESPONSE

The expression, "Women grieve; men replace," came out of the statistics of the rapid remarriage of widowers. I witnessed that in the Michigan grief seminars I helped conduct for families whose loved ones had died the previous year: Often the widows brought tissue, and the widowers brought a girlfriend or new wife.

Several years ago, *Time* magazine analyzed why widowers remarry so soon. They considered differences in physical and emotional characteristics and societal conditioning, but no firm conclusions were drawn. The following week, a woman sent the editor what I hope was a tongue-in-cheek answer: "When a man loses his wife, his work doubles. When a woman loses her husband, her work is cut in half."

Of course that may be an amusing overgeneralization, but suddenly having to do the things the spouse used to do can be overwhelming. In fact, many older women don't know how to fill the car's fuel tank. One deacon routinely asks new widows, "Do you know how to pump gas?" It's amazing the number of women, even in this modern day, who don't know how.

Often the biggest dilemma for the person wanting to assist the griever is knowing when to stop offering help. For the middle-age daughter whose bedridden mother has died, your practical help may be needed just during that busy funeral week. For the widow with young children, you may be needed to provide an emotional harbor for several weeks, until she acclimates to being on her own.

Sometimes the griever has to help set those limits. The week after Don's funeral, our neighbor Cathy sent over a lasagna dinner. I still wasn't up to cooking for just the three of us, so her offering was especially welcome. The next week, her chicken divan appeared in our kitchen.

Each time I expressed my sincere appreciation, thinking that was the end of it. When she was still sending food over during the fourth week, I knew she needed permission to stop cooking for us. I called her and tactfully let her know it was okay to stop. She sounded relieved by my call.

Often it works well for the provider to set a time limit: "For the next three weeks, I'd like to bring dinner over on Thursday nights. Would that be all right?"

DON'T EXPECT INSTANT HEALING

It amazes me how quickly our society expects us who are bereaved to get our lives back into balance. If we were baseball players and had accidents that resulted in the loss of our legs, no one would expect us to be back out in the field the next month. Losing someone—either to death or divorce—is an amputation. A special person and the life we shared are gone forever. We can't immediately jump back into the mainstream of living. Rebuilding our lives takes time.

In Ethiopia, before the dreadful famines and civil war destroyed much of that traditional culture, forty days of mourning were customary. During that time, the grieving family rested, received visitors, and ate high protein goods. On the fortieth day, they accepted gifts of fruit and roasted grain from their friends as a gentle invitation to rejoin life. Additional remembrances would be sent on the eightieth day. The first anniversary was marked by a special church service. For the next six years, the family had the option of a quiet service, taking the grain to the church and receiving personal blessings from the priests, or sending the grain with the knowledge the priests would pray for the family that day.

Keeping track of various death anniversaries, of course, was complicated, so most families had a separate book to record the dates. In our outwardly stoic, three-days-and-get-on-with-life society, it's easy to dismiss as morbid the more involved grieving of another culture. But I think the Ethiopians understand the *need* for grieving more than we do. And I'm convinced they also understand the human body's stress level better.

I learned that in a personal way. After Don died, I dumped the paperwork that could be delayed onto my writing desk until the cluttered area was an emotional weight. But I didn't have the physical energy to deal with it. Weeks passed until I had to tackle that desk just so it wouldn't torment me. So, one evening I sorted, tossed, filed, or answered every piece of paper until the desk was clear. As I admired the restored order, I picked up the calendar, wondering what day it was. It was the forty-first day after Don's death—and the first day that I had felt energetic enough to work on the project.

PREMATURE DATING

The greatest problems come when the one grieving doesn't allow enough time to work through all of the sorrow and tries to pretend that everything is normal. Many times that includes dating too soon after the death of a spouse. Just how soon is "too soon"? The "Three Cs"—Companionship, Common Interests, and Commitment—provide a good measuring stick.

People need one another, so dating fills the need of having someone to talk to. But all too often folks jump from companionship to commitment, skipping the important middle step of common interest. I saw this acted out in Don's family. I remember a relative who refused to deal with the painful emotion of his first wife's death. Instead, he met a new woman and rushed into marriage. Then a few weeks later, he seemed to awaken out of a deep sleep and discover that his first wife was dead and some stranger was sitting in her place at the table. His grief became complicated rapidly, and his anger spilled into the lives of the rest of the family.

Often a griever is startled when she finds herself attracted to someone else, especially if it's someone for whom such feelings aren't appropriate, such as her pastor or a married friend. That's such a common occurrence it even has a name: *transference*. All the energy and attention that had gone into the marriage has to go somewhere, so it's directed toward a friend or special coworker.

Misunderstood transference can tempt lonely people into making inappropriate commitments or even committing adultery. Too often we hear of a pastor who was counseling a distraught woman and then had an affair with her, destroying his marriage and ministry and causing further emotional damage for her. What the pair had accepted as love was actually transference. If they had understood it, they could have avoided its painful consequences.

HELP DEFINE NORMAL BEHAVIOR

The grief process often includes behavior so different from what the griever is used to that she may think she's losing her mind. It helps to have somebody say, "No, you're not crazy; you're grieving. This will pass."

Often grief's expression comes through temporary memory lapses. One of my friends commented that after his wife died, he found himself in a bar without remembering how he had gotten there. Normally only a social drinker, he was rightly concerned about this new behavior. Facing it and making a conscious effort to reach for the phone to call a friend—instead of grabbing the car keys—got him over the roughest time.

As we hear about situations such as the one above, it's easy to be judgmental. After all, how many times have we heard (or said) "I'd never do that"? But unless we've experienced the same tragedy, we don't know what we'd do. Remember, "Untried virtue is no virtue." How much better to say, "I *hope* I'd never do that."

ACCEPT INDIVIDUAL DIFFERENCES

Different people grieve in different ways. Some go through boxes of tissues through the roughest parts of the grieving. Others choke up, their eyes filling with tears that never fall. The problem comes when criers and non-criers judge the other's reaction to grief. I'm a crier, but at Don's funeral I concentrated on just getting through the ordeal. I knew if I started crying, I'd never be able to get through the service and the thirty-six-mile drive to the family plot for the burial. Later I made up for those dry eyes.

The following spring, though, I saw another facet of the individual differences in grief. For Memorial Day, the three of us went back to Lake Michigan, even though I wasn't sure I could face opening our summer place alone. As I pulled into the parking lot, six young neighbors to whom Don had been particularly close were hurriedly raking the leaves, trying to finish before I arrived. Their actions expressed their grief and, in effect, said, "We loved him too."

Within a few minutes, other neighbors arrived. Morrie gave me his fatherly hug and cried with me. Later Bob gestured toward the outside faucet and said, "Let's get the water turned on."

Emotional support. Practical help. Both expressions were exactly what I needed at the moment.

BE THERE

This is a scary idea for many because they think the griever's needs are limitless. But *continued* support doesn't mean *endless* support.

The greatest complaint many grievers have is: "Where are all the people who said, 'Call me anytime'?"

I remember thinking, *What they actually mean is "Call me anytime— as long as it's not too late, not during dinner or my favorite TV show, and not too often—and only in the first two weeks."*

Grievers are caught in a time warp: Each moment rolls toward us, slowly, heavily, a reminder that our life has been changed forever. But, like it or not, life does go on. The problems come when our friends expect us to move through our grief at the same rate they have moved through theirs.

REMEMBER ANNIVERSARIES AND BIRTHDAYS

The hesitancy to call attention or comment on these important dates often comes through the well-meaning statement, "But I don't want to remind her." Believe me, you're not. The very breath of the one who is mourning the death of another becomes a moment-by-moment reminder.

Jotting down the date when the person comments "Next Wednesday would have been Paulie's eleventh birthday" or "The first of next month would have been our twenty-third wedding anniversary" and then following up with a card or call—or an invitation to dinner— actually helps move the person closer to healing.

Don died less than two months before our seventeenth wedding anniversary, so the first February 5, a Saturday, loomed before me like some ancient trap door. Rose Keilhacker, a dear friend from church, invited the three of us out for lunch—and welcome conversation. With her help, I got through the day.

Anniversaries eighteen and nineteen were less traumatic because I was adjusting to widowhood. But a few weeks before the milestone of the twentieth, I wrote numerous friends and asked them to pray for me since that was the day Don had promised to ask me to marry him. Several years earlier I had realized we'd been married for more than a decade without my ever having been *asked*. In college, Don had *told* me were getting married at semester break.

When I shared my revelation, Don had grinned and said, "Well, maybe one of these days I'll ask you."

"Don! I'm serious about this," I said. "We've been married all these years and have two children. I want to be asked."

Undoubtedly he wanted to get back to the televised game. "Ooookay," he said. "Tell you what. I will—for our twentieth wedding anniversary."

He may have thought that was the end of the discussion, but I hugged thoughts of that coming milestone. Maybe we'd finally go to Scotland. We'd visit his cousins near Bathgate, touch the walls of the ancestral home, walk along the moors. He'd pick a bouquet of heather and ask me to marry him—or at least say he was glad I had married him....In reality, Don would have golfed at Saint Andrew's while I walked along the moor with his cousin Jean, but the hopeless romantic in me found comfort.

Thus, I dreaded the approach of what would have been our twentieth anniversary. Asking for help is difficult for me, but alerting several close friends to the importance of the day was the best thing I could have done. Not only did the sharing of my emotional stress actually lessen it, but I was surrounded by prayer. Many friends sent notes to encourage me, and Tedd and Ruth Bryson even added an unexpected bouquet of flowers. That emotional support helped move me on.

The evening was topped off, though, with a surprise from my then thirteen-year-old son, Jay. He made several false starts at going to bed, saying good-night at least three times. Finally, I asked, "Jay, what *is* it?" He cleared his throat, then looked at me sheepishly before saying, "Mom, will you marry my dad?"

Tears sprang to my eyes at his sweet gesture. "You bet, Jay." I finally had been asked.

GENTLY HELP THROUGH TRANSITION

If the griever is still crying after two months, don't suggest counseling and don't tell her to "get a grip." Invite her for coffee and a chat. But if she hasn't combed her hair or brushed her teeth during those two months, you might ask if she'd like to talk to someone who can help her. Again, don't overreact.

A few years ago, Dr. Canine, the counselor with whom I worked on the grief-therapy team, received a call from an adult daughter reporting her father's lack of progress and asking, "Will you see him *now?*" Months before, her mother had come home from Christmas shopping, draped her coat over the back of the chair, and toppled over with a massive heart attack.

In the days following her death, her husband refused to let anyone touch that coat. After two months, the family started calling Dr. Canine: "It's been eight weeks; you've got to do something."

He asked what other troubling things the man was doing. Nothing. He had returned to work and was still attending church. The only problem was the coat. Dr. Canine suggested they ignore it, but they called every few weeks to report that the coat was still there. And every few weeks, he suggested they ignore it.

That went on for more than eight months. Finally one August afternoon, the father picked up the coat, handed it to his daughter, and said simply, "Find someone who will need a coat this winter." When he was ready to let go, he did.

At one of my seminars, a woman asked how she could help her friend Mary, who insisted on signing her deceased husband's name to greeting cards even though he had died five years earlier. The action was giving her friends the creeps. When they asked her why she continued to do that, she replied that she didn't want their friends to forget him. And, undoubtedly, she was concerned that she might forget him too.

I suggested that she try signing only her name but adding a note such as "If Fred were here, he'd add his good wishes too."

That compromise would allow her to move forward emotionally. But it would not have happened if her friend hadn't cared enough to help.

Simple Reminders

1. God doesn't expect our smiles of acceptance in the midst of our pain.

2. We truly are "fearfully and wonderfully made." God knew what He was doing when He gave us tear ducts.

3. Job's friends sat with him for seven days and never got into trouble until they opened their mouths.

4. Be gentle with those who grieve, including yourself.

5. Grievers are caught in a time warp; each moment rolls heavily toward us as a reminder that our life has been changed forever.

7 Talking with a Child about Death
Remember to Think like a Child

The most important thing we can do for a grieving child is talk to him—and listen to his observations. Children have many questions they often can't articulate, but a concerned adult can help sort through conflicting emotions.

I learned one thing quickly: Children will have more problems if they can't cry. Ten-year-old Jay had cried as soon as I told him his dad had died, but eight-year-old Holly was in a fog for days. She even fell asleep on the way to the cemetery and was blurry-eyed at the grave-side service. The next morning she had hives so badly I kept her home from school. For much of that day, I held her on my lap even though she was eight. We both needed that closeness.

From my personal and professional experiences I've learned some important steps in helping children.

TELL THE TRUTH RIGHT AWAY

I told both children their dad had died within minutes of my return from the hospital. As difficult as that was, it gave an explanation for my tears, the overnight presence of their grandparents, the sad-faced visitors, and the endless phone calls. It also confirmed they were part of everything that touches the family.

BE TRUTHFUL

Many times a parent, thinking death is too stark for the child, gives an unhealthy explanation such as "Grandma's gone on a long trip." That's not only a lie, but it postpones having to tell the truth. Meanwhile, the child may feel resentful because Grandma didn't say good-bye.

Also, try to avoid saying such things as "Grandpa just went to sleep." Grandpa may very well have died peacefully in his sleep, but think how that sounds to a child. It isn't uncommon to have the child's sleeping patterns disturbed after a family loss as she equates sleep with death. A five-year-old may start thinking, *If I go to sleep, will I die too?*

Along with truthfulness comes the necessity of thinking the way a child does. When Carl's wife was killed in a car accident, he told three-year-old Dona her mommy was with Jesus. But when Dona's Sunday school teacher held up the traditional picture of Jesus and the children, Dona burst into tears. "Where's my mommy? My daddy said Mommy's with Jesus, but she's not there!"

While being truthful, we have to say the words "dead" and "died." But we don't like those words. We'd much rather use "fade away" or "lost" or "expired." But flowers "fade away," puppies are "lost," and parking meters "expire." People die.

I remember when my Uncle Curt died a couple of hours before I arrived at the hospital. I stood in the hallway outside his ICU cubicle, staring at the drawn blinds. I knew intellectually what the closed area meant, but I couldn't absorb the reality.

A nurse approached me and said, "Mr. Farley expired this afternoon at 4:30." I stared at her stupidly for a moment, so she repeated her news. It still didn't register right away. How much better it would have been if she had just gently said, "I'm sorry, but Mr. Farley died this afternoon."

I was so aggravated she'd used an impersonal word about my beloved uncle that when I arrived home, I looked up "expire" in the dictionary. It comes from the Latin word meaning "to breathe out." When a person dies, his last breath leaks out through his mouth, so *medically* the nurse was correct in what she said. But it sounded so impersonal.

Another inappropriate euphemism is "lost." I don't say I've "lost my husband"; my husband *died*. I'm also not one of those pious widows who says, "Oh, I haven't 'lost' my husband; I know just where he is!"

My friend Renie Smith told me about a elderly couple—I'll call them the Kidds—who used to shop at the impressive Klingman's Furniture Store in Grand Rapids, Michigan. Whenever one of their many grandchildren was about to get married, they'd venture into the store, enjoy looking at all of the displays, and then select some large item as their wedding gift. One summer it seemed as though they were in the store every few weeks, but then four, maybe five, months passed.

Finally one afternoon, their favorite clerk saw Mrs. Kidd by the clock display.

"Mrs. Kidd! How nice to see you again. How are you?"

"Oh, not very well, dear," the elderly woman replied. "I've lost my husband."

"Oh, this place is so big that happens all the time," the cheerful clerk said. "You just sit over here, and I'll have him paged. We'll find him in a jiffy."

Stunned, Mrs. Kidd could only stare at the young clerk for several moments. Finally, she managed to say, "No, dear. I mean my husband *died.*"

I'm sure neither of them forgot *that* conversation.

Part of being truthful with the child is to let him see you hurt. One of the men in our Sunday school class was killed in a car accident. His wife, left with a baby and two preteens, was so busy during the day she refused to give in to her grief until the children were asleep. As a result, they never saw her cry. That didn't translate as "strength" to her fifth grader. He interpreted it as not caring but didn't verbalize the thought until his mid-teens when he threw that perspective at her during one of their arguments.

When you share the truth about your pain, don't forget to share the truth about your comfort. Show the child the verses of Scripture that encourage you. Even preschoolers will benefit from hearing that God loves us so much He gave us verses to help us through life's tough times. My favorite passages include God's promise in Romans 8:35–39 that nothing—not even death—can separate us from His love. Psalm 23:4 helps us remember that the valley is the *shadow* of death.

First Thessalonians 4:13–18 emphasizes our hope of the resurrection. The thought that I'm going to see my beloved clown again offers enormous comfort. And even though marriages won't continue in heaven, surely I can give him an honest-to-goodness hug in greeting.

Tell Only What the Child Can Handle

Greg was pinned in the wreckage after he lost control of his car and slammed into the back of an eighteen-wheeler on a Detroit expressway. He died before the fire department could get the "Jaws of Life" machinery to the accident and before the morphine shot administered by the emergency crew could take effect. His parents wisely chose not to tell his younger brother the awful details.

I, too, initially spared Jay and Holly the details of their dad's death, telling them only that a blood clot hit his lungs and he died. Almost three years later, Jay asked if his dad had been in a lot of pain. I quoted a doctor who said that type of pulmonary embolism is just as though the "lights went out." I don't know if that's true, but I take comfort in it. I saw Don's body arch, I heard the strangling sounds (even these years later, my breathing is tense as I type this), and I know that even if the pain was intense, death came quickly. That's all I could tell Jay. And that was enough since it settled his mind on the issue.

Encourage Children to Express Feelings

Often parents are so afraid of emotion that they insist their children suppress it too. In my first experience with the death of someone I loved, I had the good fortune not to be hindered in that expression—but only because no one saw me. I was six years old when my great-grandmother Mintie Farley, or Grandma as we called her, died in

Harlan County, Kentucky. The call came at noon. After my mother hung up the phone, tears fell on her apron bib as she stirred the potatoes and onions in the iron skillet. When I asked what was wrong, she shook her head, unable to talk.

Finally I said, "Grandma died, didn't she?" I don't know where that came from. Perhaps I'd overheard one of the relatives say she was "bad off." But I ran into my parents' bedroom, sobbing as I threw myself across their white chenille bedspread. Gradually the choking in my throat eased.

But when I was sixteen, I was forced to grieve a different way. My dear elderly neighbor, Minnie Schumacher, died after a lengthy illness. I had stayed nights with her for two months after an intruder broke into her home. I was there to provide company and security for her, but she, in turn, gave me the personal attention I needed as the oldest child in a large family.

Our Saturday breakfasts in her sunny kitchen were the highlight of my week. We'd have oatmeal or eggs on her ancient, flowered china and finish the meal with cinnamon-laden hermit cookies. Over cups of green tea she'd ask about my classes and tell me about school days at the turn of the century. When she died, I felt as though I'd lost my best friend, even though there was a sixty-seven-year span between our ages.

Because of my special friendship with Miss Schumacher, her niece Doris asked me to sit with the family during the funeral. When I told a relative, he had quick advice for me: "Well, don't put on a show. You won't see those people crying and carrying on."

I certainly hadn't planned to "put on a show," but fighting back tears was too great a tension. Within two weeks, I developed deep red blotches on my face and neck. The doctor called it "some sort of reaction" and prescribed skin cream. I wish society had had a better understanding of stress-related diseases back then. Children who are allowed to express their grief not only fare better at the time but will develop stronger coping mechanisms to deal with later stress.

ALLOW CHILDREN TO ATTEND THE FUNERAL

When I worked at the funeral home, we were constantly asked if children should attend the services. We always encouraged their being included. Not only do they need to feel part of the family unit, but they also have their questions about funerals answered. Of course, I'm thinking the "normal" funeral—quiet words from the pastor, with lots of silence from the mourners that is broken only by the occasional stifled sob. If family traditions include screaming, fainting, hugging the corpse, or jumping into the grave, I wouldn't recommend that young children attend.

But while it's important they be included in the traditions, children need breaks from the intensity of the funeral home too. At one point, I looked around for Holly and discovered she was standing on tiptoe by her dad's casket, trying to warm his cold hands with her own little warm ones. I asked a relative to take both children out for a hamburger and a romp in the park.

The adults can benefit from the children's insight too. When my grandmother died in 1979, Don and I decided five-year-old Holly and six-year-old Jay would attend the funeral with us. During the drive to Kentucky, we reminded them of the biblical description of heaven, emphasizing that Mama Farley—the part we couldn't see—was already with the Lord. Then we told them about the part they would see. She'd be lying in a big box, called a casket, surrounded by flowers.

91

Many people would be in the room, we said, and some would be crying because Mama Farley couldn't talk to them anymore.

Trying to anticipate all they would see, we explained that some
people would touch her hands or kiss her forehead in the Southern
belief that such action would prevent bad dreams about the person.
We stressed that no one would make them kiss her, but they could
touch her hands if they wanted to.

We talked about the sad hymns the people would sing, what the
minister would do, and the procession of cars to the cemetery. Then,
most important of all, we asked if they had any questions. Jay was concerned with practical matters such as how the men would put the casket in the ground. But Holly merely stared at us, her eyes big with
silent wonder.

When we arrived at the funeral home, we held the children's
hands and walked into the flowered area. I studied Mama Farley's dear,
ancient face and thought of the godly example she'd been throughout
my childhood. I remembered the skinned knees and wounded pride
she had often healed with her hugs and fresh gingerbread. Still years
away in my thoughts, I was startled by Holly's question.

"Is she breathing?" she whispered.

We hadn't anticipated that one. And her question required more
than a quick no. Suddenly this business of trying to explain death to
myself had become difficult. How could I make a child understand?

"Well, Holly..." I stalled, searching for something both simple
and theologically sound.

Jay then turned from his study of the casket handles to face his
little sister. "No, Holly, she's not breathing. Remember? The breathin'
part's in heaven."

Since that April day many years ago, I've had to stand before all too many caskets. But even with tears running down my cheeks, I'm comforted as I remember a little voice confidently announcing, "The breathin' part's in heaven." If I'd had a quick answer for Holly that day, I would have missed Jay's intuitive response.

TAKE THE CHILD TO THE CEMETERY

Most of us need an object toward which we can direct our grief. If the person has already been buried, it's important that the child be taken to the grave—if he wants to go. Not only will he have his questions answered, but he gets a sense of the universality of sorrow as he sees the rows of tombstones—each one representing heartaches.

Earl was ten when his mother died. He moved through the typical haze during the preparations, but on the morning of the funeral refused to attend the service. The grandmother, concerned about how it would look to the community if he didn't attend, promptly insisted he "straighten up." A family friend wisely—and gently—stepped in, offering to stay with him. All that afternoon the two of them walked the tree-shrouded sidewalks of the village, the friend gently asking questions and encouraging the child to talk.

After several weeks of the friend's continued interest, Earl consented to visit the grave. Beneath those stately oak trees, a ten-year-old boy sobbed as the adult stood with an arm around his shoulders. Years later, as he recalled the scene, Earl expressed gratitude for the older man's understanding of a child's needs.

Not all of the grave visits will be this traumatic. Usually it merely answers questions. From childhood, my brother, sisters, and I knew Dad's father had been killed in a coal-mining accident. But it had nothing to do with us until we stood by his headstone and read the words that had been chiseled decades earlier: *We knew no sorrow, we knew no grief, till thy sweet face was missed.*

I imagined the mule-drawn wagon moving up the hill, and our dad, the somber two-year-old, watching the mysterious lowering of the wooden box into the ground. Suddenly the unknown grandfather became a person to me, and I understood my father's longing for a boyhood home. But that insight would never have come without the visit to that Kentucky hillside grave.

LET THE CHILD TALK

Even though Holly hadn't been able to cry after her dad died, she wanted to tell her classmates what had happened. Her teacher wisely allowed her to do just that. She stood in front of the class, her voice soft and her eyes downcast. Expressing her loss helped her deal with the reality of it.

How many times have we approached the adult at the funeral home and ignored the children standing nearby? It's important that they, too, be allowed to talk—to explain how their grandpa died or to share a special memory. Not only does that attention acknowledge their place in the family, but it acknowledges their grief as well.

When Ross died, his eight-year-old grandson Andy quietly tucked a picture of himself with a note in his grandpa's jacket pocket. When Marion, his grandmother, saw him, she praised his action and suggested that the other grandchildren might like to do that as well. What started as one lonesome little boy's expression of love for his grandfather became a beautiful healing activity for all of the grandchildren.

ENCOURAGE COMMUNICATION

Lack of verbalization doesn't mean lack of questions, so encourage the child to talk. Even though Jay was able to talk—and cry—about Don's death immediately, it hurt too much to ponder life without his dad, so he decided he wouldn't think about it. Complicating the situation was the comment from his schoolteacher that Jay had "settled that with the Lord" and was going on with life in a most mature way. Jay was only ten when his dad died. He hadn't "settled" anything; he was withdrawing emotionally. And I, dealing with my own grief, didn't know what was happening. He's pushed that pain so far down inside him that today, more than sixteen years after his dad's death, he doesn't have many memories of the parent with whom he most identified. Of course, I've had to deal with my guilt over not being tuned in to what was going on with my own son. But he assures me that he's okay with all this and occasionally finds my attempts to get him talking about his dad tedious. My concern is that those sad memories will bubble up once he, himself, becomes a parent.

Holly, on the other hand, allowed herself to remember her dad. And she acknowledges that not only did her dad die, but she lost the dream of what her life might have been. Major events, such as a milestone birthday, a college graduation, or a wedding, trigger that loss for her again.

BE THERE

This is the young widow's greatest complaint: "Where are all the men who said they'd help father my son?" Long ago I learned that what people think they'll do—or even wish they could do—is far different than what they can do. Having already survived numerous broken promises in my life, I took a wait-and-see attitude toward all those comments made in the funeral home.

One relative called, asking me to tell Jay and Holly he was always going to be there for them. As evidence of that, he was going to write them every week—and asked me to tell them that too. I wisely chose not to. He wrote only two notes, even after both children had expressed their appreciation. People cannot be all we want them to be—just as we can't be all they need us to be. So be careful about making impossible promises.

The need of fathering for their children is the very concern that drives many widows raising young sons alone to remarry—often with traumatic results. I remember the young widow raising a thirteen-year-old son and eight-year-old daughter alone after a tragic accident. She remarried the next year to provide a male role model, but the tension was so great between her son and new husband that she finally sent the teen to live with his widowed grandmother.

Remarriage didn't solve that situation; it merely created worse problems. Children need time to work through the depth of their loss. In the case of this young lad, he was angry because he hadn't been able to say good-bye to his father. So how could he say hello to a step-father?

Meeting that need for fathering is where the church can make a major difference in a child's life. I'm not suggesting that one man absorb all of the responsibility, but if several deacons or the father's friends would include the son even once a month with their own family, it would make a world of difference in how the boy sees himself. I'm thankful for two of our friends who did invite Jay to a football game and a camping weekend. And I'm realistic enough to know the extra effort it took to include an outsider. I especially appreciate it because I found it so hard to ask for help.

I remember the father/son banquet we had at our church. Since several sports figures, including a Detroit Pistons basketball star, were going to be there, Jay casually mentioned he wanted to go. I couldn't ask one of our friends to include Jay because I knew they'd want to enjoy the special evening with their own sons. And I didn't blame them.

Since I wasn't into Rent-a-Boyfriend, I had no choice but to take Jay myself. Being the only woman in attendance at an all-male event didn't bother me until we walked into the hall, and I realized we didn't have assigned seats. I would have to approach a table full of men and ask if we could join them. Argh!

With shaking knees, I put on my brightest smile, approached an available table, and asked, "Are you gentlemen secure enough to allow a woman to sit at your table?" (I cringe now to think of that statement, but it was produced by fear rather than arrogance.) They laughed and welcomed us, and I got through the evening. Later, one of the leaders, who had been a friend of Don's, came to me. "It really hit me when I saw you walk into the room with Jay," he said. "I'm so sorry I didn't think about the fatherless boys in time to do anything for them this year."

Well, the next year, the leaders had again forgotten. That time I planned a special out-of-town trip for the three of us.

AFFIRM THE CHILD'S FEELINGS

The most common adult reaction to a child's expression of an emotion other than sadness is "Don't feel like that!" Normal emotions may include anger—even at the deceased parent—guilt, and relief. Adults' negative responses add greater turmoil to children's unvoiced emotions. Children don't conjure up these feelings; they just *have* them.

Two weeks after Don's death, we three were driving to the church for the midweek service. In the silence, Holly suddenly said, "I'm so angry!"

Anger was not what I wanted to hear right then. I was missing Don, convinced I couldn't raise our children without his laughter and not at all sure I was going to survive my own grief. In the midst of all that, I was supposed to continue teaching, pay bills, and be the strong person everyone thought I was. But that night I was too tired to say anything other than, "Who are you angry at, Holly?"

She didn't answer for a long moment, so I said, "Are you angry with God for letting your daddy die?"

Long silence again. Finally she mumbled, "No."

"It's okay if you are angry at Him," I said.

More silence, then she said, "No. 'Cause He helps us."

We stopped at the light at Lilly and Joy roads. "Are you angry at your daddy?" I asked.

Only silence came from the backseat, so I tried again. "He didn't want to leave, honey," I said. "He did everything he could to stay with us. He wanted to watch you and Jay grow up."

"I know." More silence, then, "I'm not angry at him."

"Well, do you know who you are angry at?" I held my breath. Surely she was angry at me since I was supposed to be taking care of her dad. Instead she gave one of her exasperated sighs.

"I'm angry at Adam and Eve. None of this would have happened if they hadn't disobeyed God!"

Her solution may seem rather simplistic, but it gave her someone she could direct that anger toward. Being able to verbalize pain is the first step toward resolving it. That sounds rather easy, but for many families any display of emotion is the same as "loss of control." But by helping the child deal with rampant emotions today, we have strengthened the future adult.

Simple Reminders

1. Children have questions they often can't articulate, but a concerned adult can help them sort through conflicting emotions.

2. Avoid giving a dishonest explanation of the death such as "Grandma's gone on a long trip."

3. Even preschoolers will benefit from hearing that God loves us so much He gave us verses to help us through life's tough times.

4. Children who are allowed to express their grief not only fare better at the time but will develop stronger coping mechanisms to deal with later stress.

5. Older children should be allowed to attend the funeral. Not only do they need to feel part of the family unit, but they also need their questions about funerals answered.

6. If you say you're going to "be there" for a grieving family, make sure you follow through on your word.

7. If well-meaning people forget the promises they've made to you in the funeral home, try to remember they cannot be all we want them to be—just as we can't be all they need us to be.

8 *Abnormal Grief*

Don't Get Stuck in Unhealthy Grief

Normal grief is painful enough, but when it is combined with grief that is chronic, delayed, exaggerated, or masked, it becomes all the more intense. Let's look at those areas of abnormal grief and their resulting complications.

CHRONIC

Chronic grief is constant and overwhelming—and goes on for weeks, perhaps even months. The grieving parent may not be able to take over the care of her young children yet. If she is older, perhaps she still can't get dressed, brush her teeth, or comb her hair without someone directing her every move. "No, Ma. Your arm goes here."

If this behavior happens for the first couple of weeks following the death, it's not unusual and is still part of the initial stage in which everything seems to move in slow motion. The griever may even feel that others' voices are coming from the end of a long tunnel. All of that is normal. But if this behavior persists, then it's time for direct action on the part of those around the griever.

That loving intervention primarily comes in the form of other survivors taking the newest one by the hand and showing her it is possible to go on. Sometimes all it takes is another widow staying with her for a couple of days and occasionally saying, "It's time to get dressed now."

While most people move through even this intense stage eventually, it still may take professional intervention via a knowledgeable grief therapist. Usually though, it comes through some sudden realization. Some of the young widows I talked to mentioned the feeling of awakening from a bad dream, realizing their children had gone to school that morning but not knowing who had gotten breakfast for them. Concern for the children is often the triggering factor.

When my Grandpa Ted Picklesimer was only twenty-two, he died after his right leg was crushed by a coal-mining car. His children were four years (Aunt Reva), two years (my dad), and six weeks (Uncle Ishmael). After the funeral, my Grandma Katie "took to her bed"—as we say in the South. She literally collapsed and had no strength to move or to care for her children.

The women in that little mountain valley took turns caring for the children, but she was so despondent they thought they'd soon bury her. They'd seen that happen before.

One morning, her father, Big John T. Dunn burst into her bedroom. "Katie, if you die, too, who's gonna take care of these younguns?"

Her eyes opened wide. Immediately she swung her feet onto the floor and took the baby from the hovering neighbor. Her father left as quickly as he had arrived; his daughter was going to be just fine. Not only did she allow the Lord to rebuild her life, but years later she would be my example when my own widowhood seemed overpowering.

DELAYED

This is the most common abnormal grief response. The manifestation of this response is usually calm, even magnificent acceptance of the tragedy at the time of its occurrence. At the funeral home, he quotes the right Scriptures and actually comforts those who came to comfort him. But months later, when everyone else has gotten on with their lives, he falls apart. He may become a real pain, picking fights with everyone over the least thing, demanding his way in inappropriate areas. Or he may become so deeply depressed he can't function.

This type of abnormality also shows up when the grief has been postponed, as, for example, until after a court settlement. Grief therapists all have stories of parents who went through a court battle after the death of a child. The battle may have dragged on for three years, with the parents concentrating upon the procedure. Once the case was settled however, the grief was allowed to surface and was as intense as if the child had died three days earlier instead of three years ago.

The grief also may be delayed if the death occurred during the survivor's childhood, and she was not allowed to grieve then. One of my friends, whom I'll call Teri, was five when her parents were killed in a train accident. Her grandmother, who never showed her own grief, didn't allow the little girl to go to the funeral, saying it was no place for children.

For all of the years Teri lived with her grandmother, her parents were never again mentioned. On the surface, she had adjusted well. But when she married, she panicked so profoundly each time her husband had to be away on business that she finally sought professional help.

When the therapist asked about her parents, Teri sobbed throughout the session, remembering that frightened five-year-old who didn't understand what had happened. Her assignment that week was to talk to two aunts and find out the details. Once she was allowed to grieve, she could finally move on with the rest of her life—without the obsession that her husband was going to leave her too.

This delayed grief can also surface years after a miscarriage or an abortion, which we'll talk about in chapter 11.

EXAGGERATED

Often the survivor doesn't want to talk about the person who has died but becomes obsessed with the subject of death and dying. He may collect Victorian funeral jewelry, read books on world funeral customs, or take classes on death and dying, supposedly to help others who are hurting. Certainly some of this is normal curiosity and honest attempts at easing the pain of others. But if he prefers to talk about the world's loss rather than his personal one, it may take gentle questions about his family member or friend to help him sort through the details of his specific grief.

When I worked for a funeral home as a community service representative, I often spoke to small groups within the town. I remember one widow's group where most of the women started passing the tissue box as soon as I introduced myself. My plan for the evening was to direct their thinking into ways they could use personal hurt to help others. They also could share some of the things they had learned from their pain. One woman insisted she was in the group just to give her some place to go each month. She kept concentrating upon the grief of others but refused to say anything about her own loss.

After the meeting, she inquired about the possibility of working for our funeral home. "Dead people just fascinate me," she said. I didn't encourage her to apply.

Another acquaintance celebrated each special anniversary associated with his mother—her birthday, date of cancer diagnosis, and date of death—with the purchase of a Victorian funeral photo or Victorian funeral jewelry. The jewelry, often a brooch with a picture of the deceased (either when alive or actually in the casket) along with a lock of hair, are difficult to find, so the gathering of each purchase was an adventure in itself and, in fact, seemed to be his life's goal. He never mentioned his mother and refused to talk about her even when friends mentioned a special memory they had of her. His collection had become a substitution for facing his personal grief.

MASKED

This response is similar to our society's custom of avoidance and denial. In this, the personhood of the survivor isn't strong enough to cope with his loss, so he must mask his pain in order to continue living. One of Don's relatives returned from his wife's funeral and insisted his adult children and their spouses get rid of her jewelry and clothing within the hour. They were astonished. They were just barely coping with their own grief; how could he be so strong?

Within two months, it was evident he wasn't propelled by

strength at all. Not only was this former church deacon suddenly hanging out in the local bars, but he persuaded his new girlfriend to winter in Florida with him less than three months after his wife's death. His family was horrified—and more than a little angry. How could he do this to their mother's memory? How could he decide not to live by the same rules he had always insisted his sons live by? What had happened to the dad they knew?

And that's the whole point. Since he couldn't cope with the reality of his loss, he had to mask it and become someone they didn't know. The one they knew wasn't as strong as they had thought. He knew that, too, and had to substitute another, lesser set of principles in order to face the pain of his wife's death.

Another route this masking can take is that the person becomes self-centered. The pain he is trying to hide is so great he doesn't have room for anyone else's pain. But rather than say, "I can't handle that; I have enough problems of my own," he will mask it with harshness. Barbara recalls her father's response to their neighbor's accident: "Anybody who doesn't have the sense to stay off the roads on Memorial Day deserves just what he got."

Any of these inappropriate responses can result in greater problems later. As searing as fresh grief is, the recovery still is swifter when we face our loss.

Simple Reminders

1. Normal grief is painful enough, but when it is combined with grief that is chronic, delayed, exaggerated, or masked, it becomes all the more intense.

2. Chronic grief is constant and overwhelming—and can go on for weeks, perhaps even months.

3. Delayed grief is the most common abnormal grief response and often is manifested through calm, even magnificent acceptance of the tragedy at the time of its occurrence.

4. Exaggerated grief often results in the survivor's not wanting to talk about the person who has died but becoming obsessed with the general subject of death and dying.

5. Masked grief is similar to our society's custom of avoidance and denial.

9 Coping with Normal Depression
Pushing Away Emotional Clouds

One of the most common results of grief is depression. It often originates in physical illness, guilt, giving up, self-effort, wrong perspective, adjustment reactions, and/or learned behavior. As we talk about these conditions, I want to stress that depression is not something "to snap out of," especially when it's clinical or caused by a chemical imbalance. If a family member is still depressed several months after a family death, by all means make an appointment with the doctor. His counsel and perhaps even simple medication often help quickly.

PHYSICAL ILLNESS

The caregiver of an ill person battles the disease right along with the patient and often winds up with his/her own physical problems.

This is one of those "Which came first, the chicken or the egg?" situations. Do we become ill because we're depressed? Or do we become depressed because we're ill?

We do know stress lowers our body's ability to fight disease. We can all think of cases where a seemingly strong, healthy widow died from breast cancer or a heart attack the year after her husband died. It's even more common for the survivor to have lowered resistance and to catch every possible germ. The illness that develops from stress is real—it's not something we dream up to gain sympathy.

My stress during Don's illness managed to burn out some central core, allowing lupus—an internal cousin to arthritis—to come swooping in shortly after his death. Mine was stress induced, so my internist, who first suggested chemotherapy (No, thanks! I refused to have Jay and Holly watch a parent go through that again.), and I have agreed that, for now, mine is controllable with rest and proper nutrition. I'm thankful for the progress I've made. I remember the symptoms that began during the nights of getting up to give Don his medication and having to grip the wall as I walked because of the pain in my legs and feet.

Not being able to continue with usual activities certainly causes depression and creates more stress. Doris Schumacher, my dear ninety-five-year-old friend, has lost the two activities she most enjoyed—walking and reading—because of her deteriorating eyesight. She was the one whose example years ago encouraged me to get an education. Now she's teaching me how to grow old. Together we lament what she has lost, but then she quickly reminds me she has much to be thankful for. It sounds simplistic, but by concentrating on what she can still enjoy—phone chats, visits with friends, and hours in a sunny courtyard—she continues to fight the depression that could easily envelop her.

GUILT

We discussed the three types of guilt—true, false, and misplaced—at length in a previous chapter, but I want to emphasize here their impact upon depression.

I'm one of those who can handle a crisis but can't handle guilt. I learned a long time ago I might as well give in to a family member rather than suffer guilt for days (weeks!) afterward. Example: It's late Friday afternoon years ago in Michigan. I'm adding the final corrections for the article that must be in the 5:00 P.M. mail. Then after a nice dinner with Jay and Holly, I'm planning to work on the grief seminar I'm presenting at a local church the next morning. I'm especially looking forward to going to bed early. Then the phone rings.

"Are you busy, honey?" It's my dear mother.

"Never too busy to talk," I confess. "What's happening?"

"Well, your uncle arrived this afternoon."

"Oh, that's great. I didn't know he was coming this way. Maybe we can stop in Sunday afternoon to say hello."

"Well, honey," she begins, and my stomach knots. "He's going to be here just for tonight. He leaves tomorrow for his daughter's home."

I glance at the corrections still to be made on the article. No, I'm going to be tough this time. "Oh, I'm sorry I'm going to miss him, but I'm swamped," I reply. "Tell him we'll catch him the next time."

Sigh. Pause. Do I hear her wiping tears from her eyes before she speaks? "Well, honey, I don't know if there will be a 'next time.' He hasn't been feeling well lately."

She has won. "Set three more plates, Mother," I say. "We'll be there in two hours."

Most of us can relate to such scenes and may even chuckle over them. But guilt can keep us trapped in depression unless we take certain steps to free ourselves.

The first step in being free of the power of guilt is to recognize it. If we ignore it, we're allowing it to silently grow.

Next, accept it as a universal problem. You're not the first, nor will you be the last, to struggle in this area.

Finally, find ways to let it go. Some may have to remind themselves they can't do everything and have to choose the most important. Some may need to concentrate on the fact they made their decision based on the information they had at the time. Still others may have to face their true guilt, confess it, and let it go.

When I've confessed my guilt but still have trouble letting it go, I quote 1 John 1:9 to myself: "If we confess our sins, he is faithful and just to forgive us our sins, and to cleanse us from all unrighteousness" (KJV). If Almighty God, in His perfection, will forgive imperfect me as I ask, I'd be foolish to reject that gift.

GIVING UP

At first, our giving in to times of depression may be our choice, but as the patterns are repeated, the brain releases toxins that can set us up for deeper problems.

Don gave in to total depression for one day, refusing to talk, and concentrating only on the doctors' ominous diagnosis. The next morning he said, "Well, I tried being bummed yesterday, and it was so horrible I'm not going to be depressed again. I guess I'll just have to show these doctors they're wrong." And that was when they were saying he had as few as two weeks to live!

So I continue to ponder these questions: How much of Don's

extra time was due to this personal fight, and how much was God's intervention? If I give more credit to Don, am I taking away from God's miracle? Or if I give all the credit to God, am I denying the power of the personal fight? If so, then I'm heaping guilt on those who truly want to get well but can't.

Obviously, I don't have the answers, but I know the One who does. And it's all right to ask as long as we're willing to listen to His answers.

SELF-EFFORT

This is the feeling that we must do everything ourselves—a conviction that weighs heavily on the shoulders of many. Believe it or not though, ladies, the Superwoman image is no longer popular. We don't have to do everything. And the same goes for you men. Not even the broadest shoulders were made to carry everything.

I remember feeling as though nothing would get done if I didn't do it. But all of my self-effort was pulling energy—and joy—out of me. In fact, on my fortieth birthday, friends teased me about being "over the hill." But I welcomed the milestone. "Hey, I'm glad to be this age," I said. "When I was in my thirties I was always trying to prove something to someone. Now I'm free to be exactly who I am." I had finally learned that even self-effort doesn't erase some challenges. Today, I confess that the only thing I miss about my youth is the skin. I wouldn't want to have to go through all of those struggles again.

As we get older, we understand that freedom comes when we don't play games—and when we don't try to carry all those burdens ourselves. If we allow Him to, the Lord helps us through this thing loosely called "life." We don't have to carry our burdens alone—and we don't have to be everything to everybody.

We're at our best when we're allowed to use our skills. God has given us different talents, but too often we limit ourselves. If we can't balance the checkbook to the penny, we think we're stupid. If we can't play the piano or speak in front of large groups, we think God doesn't have a spot for us in His kingdom. That's wrong thinking that can lead us into greater emotional problems, including depression.

WRONG PERSPECTIVE

It's important that we talk to others to get their point of view.

In the weeks following Don's death, memories of his dying tormented me. As his back arched, I—the doer and the supposedly strong one—had been relieved that the doctors rushed past me to assist him. Obviously, I'd watched too many Hollywood scenes of the wife cradling the husband, whispering words of comfort and strength. Real deathbed scenes aren't always so peaceful, and I was tormented by my uselessness.

During a call from our friends Morrie and Gert Driesenga, they asked a sincere, "How are you doing?" I cried as I expressed my frustration. Morrie spoke first and gave me the different perspective I needed: "You didn't abandon him. You got out of the way so those who knew what to do could help."

He offered a simple statement, but his words carried profound comfort.

ADJUSTMENT REACTIONS

In the face of stress, we have to adjust or we'll get depressed. My motto for both my professional and personal schedule is "analyze and adjust." Neither my health nor my sanity will allow me to accomplish everything I want to do or even should do, so I adjust by setting priorities. What has to be finished today? What can wait until next week?

During one of my busiest weeks back in New York, I was typing like crazy, trying to finish a writing deadline before leaving to speak at a writers' conference, when Jay, who was then a teenager, called me downstairs. The outside panel of our thermal sliding door had suddenly and inexplicably shattered.

When I saw the glass, I gasped first. We're all allowed to do that! Then I examined the door and discovered the second panel was intact; it would hold until after I'd taken care of the other obligations.

How does this relate to grief? We have to adjust to all of the new responsibilities suddenly thrust upon us. When Don died, my grief was compounded by single parenting, and I wanted to run away to Tahiti—or Kentucky. But one of my friend's comments gave me the proper perspective: "Just keep the kids clean and fed; the rest of it can wait."

LEARNED BEHAVIOR

Our children learn how to handle stress by watching the adults in their lives—just as we learned in the same way. My mother would have reacted to that New York shattered door in the same way I did—gasp, examine it, sigh, and go on with her activities until she could do something about it.

Others would have turned the situation into a major crisis. I remember the noon one of my cousins burst into our kitchen. She had run from her house—several blocks away. All she could sob was something about "water" and "ceiling."

My mother drove her home to see what the problem was. The

faucet on the basement pipes had jarred open, spraying water. Mother shut off the water and then brought the still whimpering bride back to our place for lunch.

Both my mother and my cousin had reacted as they had seen their own mothers react in similar situations. But I'm thankful we don't have to be bound by our early environment. And we don't have to be overcome by depression—even in the midst of grief.

Simple Reminders

1. Depression is not something to snap out of, especially when it's clinical or caused by a chemical imbalance.

2. Concentrating on what we have left instead of what we have lost helps ward off depression.

3. The first step in being free from the power of guilt is to recognize it. If we ignore it, we're allowing it to silently grow.

4. We don't have to be overcome by depression—even in the midst of grief.

5. We don't have to carry our burdens alone—and we don't have to be everything to everybody.

6. In times of stress, we have to adjust or we'll become depressed. Start by asking yourself, "What has to be finished today? What can wait until next week?"

7. Our children learn how to handle stress by watching the adults in their lives.

10 Coping with the Death of a Child
A Loving Parent's Greatest Fear

One of our local cemeteries contains the grave of little Casey Jane Troupe, who was barely twenty-two months old when she died. The front of her tombstone bears her name and nickname—"Boots"—as well as the full dates of her birth and death.

I happened to be standing by that tiny grave as I waited for another interment service to begin. To make room for the other folks who were arriving, I stepped behind the little girl's stone where, on the back, I discovered this poem:

> "Come on, come on" you called to us.
>   "I want you to be near.
> "Come on, come on, come be with me"
>   You said when you were here.

We hear you still sweet Casey Jane
    calling from above.
You gently call "Come on" again
    So softly now, with love.
We love you, and we miss you so,
    And though we know not when,
Our Lord has made a promise that
    We'll be with you again.
So keep calling to us, Casey;
    His promise will come true.
And from that day we'll get to spend
    Eternal life with you.

There in the Colorado sun, I read the words as tears filled my eyes. I nudged a friend who stood next to me then motioned toward the poem.

He nodded. "I know," he said. "How would you stand it?"

After a little investigation, I later contacted the mother of that precious little girl to tell her of my appreciation for the beautiful expression of so short a life. The mother, Katie, graciously consented to talk about their Casey Jane who is forever locked in their hearts as a twenty-two-month-old toddler instead of the five-year-old "big sister" she should be to the younger children.

As Katie told the tragic circumstances of the bubbly child having been hit by a car, I asked about the nickname. The mother's voice was soft with the remembering.

"Her daddy called her that," she said and then told of an uncle who had sent a box of clothes that his daughter had outgrown. In the package was a pair of bright pink snow boots, which Casey insisted upon pulling on immediately, even though it was summer. With glee, she had proclaimed her find with a two-syllable pronunciation: "Boots-sa!" Her dad immediately had latched on to her sweet way of saying it by nicknaming her "Boots."

My heart breaks for all that this young couple—and their extended family—have suffered. Does a loving parent or grandparent have any greater fear than the death of a child? After all, it is contrary to our concept of the way things should be: Our children should someday bury us, not the other way around.

A Special Pain

All of the grief principles I've listed in earlier chapters can be applied to the death of a child. But I'm convinced that this special grief carries even greater pain. After all, the parents have lost part of their future. With this child, there will be no graduations, no wedding plans, no grandchildren. In the case of an only child, there's no one to give Grandma's wedding quilt to, no one to carry on the stories of Grandpa's faith during a family crisis.

As a single parent, I think how much more difficult it would be to have to bear that terrible load alone. One of my friends said that at least when her son died, she was able to cling to her husband as they sobbed together. She said she couldn't imagine how she would have gotten through the first few months after their child's death if it hadn't been for her husband.

Grieving parents are often left out of other family's celebrations. After all, the thought is, joyful celebrations of graduations and weddings remind the grieving parents of what they have lost. But how much better to extend the invitation and let them decide if they want to attend. If they do, acknowledge their child with a gentle private word or, as appropriate, a public display.

A couple of years ago, one of the young women from my son's college class was brutally raped and murdered after being randomly selected at a stoplight and followed to an apartment parking lot. Several weeks later, on a beautiful spring day with Pikes Peak in the background, the diplomas were presented alphabetically to the graduating class. Partway through the list, the master of ceremonies announced that the mother of the murdered girl would accept her diploma. Immediately the audience of three thousand sprang to their feet and tearfully applauded the mother for several minutes. The horrible crime couldn't be undone, but the crowd was acknowledging the unspeakable wrong that had stolen her vivacious daughter.

IMPORTANT SUGGESTIONS

Often that all-important acknowledgment of the dead child helps a parent through the dark days. But sometimes parents have to let their friends know how they can help.

Barb and Bob Reynolds, along with their daughter, Robin, sent the following Christmas letter three months after the bicycle accident that claimed the life of their eighteen-year-old son, Corey:

> Dear Family and Friends:
>
> We have become painfully aware that our society leaves very little room for prolonged mourning or thoughts outside of the scope of living. Yet with each new day, our minds are never far from the life and death of our son and brother, Corey Robert Reynolds. While many of you have openly expressed

your sorrow over Corey's tragic accident, there are those of you who still have difficulty talking about him now that he is dead. Today's society typically allows only a few weeks to share in a loss, and then expects us to "move on" with the business of living.

Let us tell you, gently, that from our experience it is simply not that easy! In order for us to "move on," we must leave a special place in our hearts and minds to reflect on the precious memories of our dear Corey. And we think about him *every single day*. So please allow us to share our thoughts on how we would welcome you to talk with us about our precious son:

- Please do not be embarrassed by bringing up the subject of Corey's accidental death. We will be glad to share with you exactly what happened.
- We know that you can't say "I understand how you feel" unless you have also lost a child, and even then it's different for everyone. It's not at all like losing your mother, father, or grandparents. However, do feel free to tell us that you are sorry and that you care.
- Do not feel as if you have to avoid mentioning Corey or his death in order not to make us sad. We long for opportunities to talk about and remember him, and it is often difficult for us to initiate such a discussion or know who it is "safe" to do so with. Sometimes we just need someone to listen. We are grateful when you provide an opening or remind us that you are available.
- We visit our son's grave as often as we can—it helps to comfort us. We welcome you to visit also. Many things

trigger our tears, often just the thought of life without Corey. Tears are normal. This is one way we grieve his loss.

- Please share any stories or memories with us you may have about Corey. We are trying to collect them in a memorial scrapbook about his life. While it is sometimes painful, we love reminiscing about him.

We are grateful that God gave us eighteen and a half precious years with Corey. It was too short on *our* timeline, and yet *God's* timing is always perfect. We will never forget the gift of our son, and we hope his memory will remain as strong in your hearts as it will in ours.

Like so many others who grieve, Barb uses journalizing and poetry writing to release some of the pent-up pain over the death of their six-foot-nine-inch son. She wrote the following poem for Corey's funeral bulletin:

Our Tribute to Our Son and Brother

Oh! How we remember you!
Your hair so red and eyes so blue.
Your goofy grin and stubbly chin,
The way you looked when you walked in.
We remember you as small,
And then you grew so very tall.
We didn't mind, no not one bit
Although your shoes were hard to fit,
And sometimes clothes were hard to buy,
But that's okay—you were our tall guy.

Even as a man full-grown,
> Your purity and innocence brightly shone.

You knew the Lord—how glad we are—
> And even though you now seem far

Away from us, we do know
> That someday, we too shall go

And see you there with your red hair
> And eyes so blue—Oh! How we remember you!

You brought to us such love and joy,
> We miss you dearly, our big boy.

A NEW DEFINITION OF NORMAL

In Rebecca Faber's book *A Mother's Grief Observed*, she writes about how the drowning of eighteen-month-old William affected her family:

> We are all changed forever. We are disabled as a family. The death of a child is an amputation—forced removal of limb, an organ. How does a person learn to live without a leg or an eye? You can. You must. But it is not *normal*. What you move toward is a new definition of *normal*. We say, "She's a quadriplegic—but she taught herself how to write and draw with her mouth." Or "He's lost a leg—he's handicapped." These things become "normal life" for that person. But normal now includes un-normal twisting, crippling, a truncation felt minute after minute, hour after hour. Enormous adjustments are required. How can we keep from bitterness? How can we create joy and gratitude in the new "normal" life?

So we must develop a new family life—fresh patterns will emerge. And I have to get more organized....Children need to know what they can rely on, day by day. They love repetition. They count on it.

We need order, and we need hope.[1]

THE COMPASSIONATE FRIENDS POEM

In their 1997 Christmas letter, Barb Reynolds also included this poem written by John and Bonnie Challis from the Winnipeg chapter of The Compassionate Friends—an international support group for grieving families:

We Do Not Need a Special Day

We do not need a special day
To bring you to our minds.
The days we do not think of you
Are very hard to find.

Each morning when we awake,
We know that you are gone.
And no one knows the heartache
As we try to carry on.

Our hearts still ache with sadness,
And secret tears still flow.
What it meant to lose you
No one will ever know.

Our thoughts are always with you.
Your place no one can fill.

In life we loved you dearly,
In death we love you still.

There will always be a heartache,
And often a silent tear,
But always a precious memory
Of the days when you were here.

If tears could make a staircase,
And heartaches make a lane,
We'd walk the path to Heaven
And bring you home again.

We hold you close within our hearts,
And there you will remain,
To walk with us throughout our lives
Until we meet again.

Our family chain is broken now,
And nothing seems the same,
But as God calls us one by one,
The chain will link again.[2]

SPECIAL CHALLENGES

A couple whom I'll call Russell and Elizabeth lead a group for grieving parents in their Midwest church. In addition to providing a safe gathering for tears and stories, they also let the parents know that their special challenges are not uncommon as they share their own adjustments to life after the death of their eight-year-old daughter.

One major point that Russell makes early is that men and women often grieve differently. Many times, a man will not express his thoughts and will busy himself at work, sometimes hiding in overtime. Often the wife wants to talk about the child and wants to remember specific scenes with him—as though by her very words she can hold him again. The father may not like the emotions that well up within him during those moments, so he doesn't want to revisit those scenes.

Elizabeth talks about how even the couple's lovemaking can be affected. Again, each case is different. Some grieving fathers see that activity as affirmation of life itself and turn to their wives even more. Some husbands distance themselves, leaving their wives feeling all the more abandoned. The problems of course increase when the couple is not communicating what the lovemaking represents for them individually.

For example, if the father wants that closeness as an affirmation of life as well as love for his wife, she may be thinking, *How can I enjoy that when our child is lying cold and still in the ground?* The important thing is that each couple must communicate during this difficult time and explain to the other what their lovemaking means.

As Russell and Elizabeth stress that this is not the time to try to guess what your partner is feeling, they always notice relieved glances passing between the couples in the group.

They also talk about what to do with the child's room. Some parents move to a new home where they won't have to face the memory of the child in every corner. Others want to stay in the home that once sheltered their child. The important thing, they say, is to be where you are the most comfortable.

Many parents ask them how to answer the eventual question "How many children do you have?" Elizabeth remembers wondering if she should say two, thereby ignoring their daughter. But if she said three and folks later saw only two at church, they would be confused. Finally, she settled on an explanation that said it all: "Two sons here on earth and a daughter in heaven."

This is an area where our personal faith especially helps as we look forward to being reunited with that dear child again. On the tough days, that's our greatest hope.

Simple Reminders

1. The death of a child is contrary to our concept of the way things should be: Our children should someday bury us, not the other way around.

2. Through the death of a child, parents have lost part of their future. With this child, there will be no graduations, no wedding plans, no grandchildren.

3. The tendency is not to include the grieving parents in family celebrations because we don't want to "remind them."

4. Don't tell grieving parents "I understand how you feel" unless you have also lost a child.

5. Encourage the parents to share their memories of the child. Share any that you have with them too.

11 *Thoughts on Miscarriage and Abortion*

More Lives Ending Too Soon

Many miscarriages happen early in pregnancy, just as the expectant mother is beginning to smile in that secret way as she sees other pregnant women or newborn babies in the shopping center. She has imagined a future with this child growing and laughing and causing her to see the world in a new way—even though he weighs only a few ounces at the present. Then suddenly the cramps and the stains announce that the dream is lost along with that child, and she is thrust into deep grief even though others were not even aware of the child's existence. For the mother, the miscarriage was not a potential child but an actual one. And the death of this baby can taint the excitement of the next pregnancy because she and her husband know what can happen.

ONE WOMAN'S STORY

One of my Ohio cousins, Trish Colby, and her husband, Rick, have three beautiful little girls, but they experienced two miscarriages between the births of their first two daughters, Ashley and Rachel.

Trish was twelve weeks along with the first miscarriage. The second one occurred at eight weeks. And even there, the situations were different. With Trish's first miscarriage, she didn't even spot. In the second one, she woke up covered with blood. During the first miscarriage, she had known intuitively that something was wrong. Sure enough, after the ultrasound, the doctor matter-of-factly told them the baby was dead and that she could just go home and await "nature's course." Trish tearfully said she could not leave with a dead baby in her and asked for another alternative. The doctor scheduled an immediate D and C.

But each woman's needs are different, and one of Trish's friends, facing the same situation, went home, comforted that she had her baby within her for even those few more hours.

After the procedure, Trish's doctor said, "One in four women have these. Go home and try again. This is no big deal."

But, of course, it was a big deal. Trish says, "A miscarriage is like a present that will never be unwrapped."

Complicating her grief were the thoughtless things people said, including "Well, you weren't really that far along. It isn't as though you lost a real baby."

But the child was real to her.

Vickie's aunt met the news that her niece had miscarried her third child with a shrug and the comment, "Well, you didn't need another mouth to feed anyway."

Such comments make the mother feel all the more alone when she, in fact, needs others to care that she is going through such a difficult time.

Trish is a political consultant, so she's surrounded by professional, educated women, many of whom have miscarried and are still in great emotional pain.

"Too many people look at our business suits and think we should be fine by tomorrow. Well, we're not fine tomorrow or next week."

The one thing that did help Trish was to come home from the hospital to another child. "Holding Ashley helped me," Trish says. "You don't want to let that little one that you do have out of your sight. People—even husbands—don't realize how much grief there is because we aren't showing yet, but it's real to the mother. We are already starting to dream. What will he or she look like? What will his personality be like? If you lose that dream, it's hard to come to grips with it."

She continues, "This is like breast cancer was years ago—afterward you just hide in your house and hurt. One in four women have miscarriages; one in nine women have breast cancer. And it does affect more than just the mother. There's loss of productivity at work, and marriages can break up, so it has long-range effects."

Often, the husband's way of coping is to shut down emotionally. One young wife explains it this way: "Husbands want to fix things; but they can't fix this, so they want to withdraw. Women often need to talk about it and talk about it. Husbands say in effect to their wives, 'I can't deal with this. Each time you talk about it, I have to go through it again, and I can't do that.'"

Trish found that even if her friends would just sit with her and nod, they were helping. She further adds, "I would have liked some-one to meet me at the hospital to talk to me about what I was feeling and what I would experience in the days ahead. Later, I didn't find much useful information at the library. It was all too impersonal, too technical."

She pauses, remembering. "I felt so all alone. It's easier to cope when you know someone else has gone through the same ordeal. Women need to talk to another woman. The secrets come out only once you've miscarried. It's a secret society."

Kari remembers a friend who miscarried at four months. "The morning after she arrived home, I watched her look through the hos-pital in-patient bag," Kari says. "And it was as though she thought she'd find the baby if she just looked hard enough. It struck me as really weird, and I didn't like being around her. Later I wrote her, after my own miscarriage, and told her I'd had no idea of the pain she was going through. I'd thought she was weird, but later she was the only one who could help me."

Marilee says, "I wish I could have talked to my husband about this, but the coping mechanisms for men and women are very differ-ent. It helped that I had other friends who had gone through this."

Trish says, "It is hard when people ask how we're doing, and it's hard when they don't. It all depends on the person who is asking. Here we are, hard-core women in politics—many of us have experi-enced being the only woman in the boardroom—yet we want to talk about our baby's death. Often we have convinced ourselves that we can handle anything, then this thing smacks us in the face and we can't fix it."

A Plea for More Research

"Rick and I are the miscarriage poster people of the Columbus area," Trish says. "We're in the process now of setting up a foundation to help others facing this same trauma."

They had hoped to run their foundation through the hospital but are finding they may have to set it up as a private foundation and raise money through research companies.

"Ohio is looking into a miscarriage registry to gather family history—such as eating and work habits and closeness to harmful industries—to trace patterns," Trish says. "Having a hunch is one thing, but proving it is another."

At present, very little data on what causes miscarriages is available. Not knowing a cause can be very difficult. After all, it's human nature to want to know why something bad happened so we can avoid it next time.

Trish agrees. "The guilt is intense: 'If only I hadn't had that second cup of coffee. If only I hadn't worked that extra hour.' Through research, we've learned the importance of taking folic acid to prevent birth defects, and we now have steroid shots for the baby that will almost double the lung capacity for an impending early birth. But we need more answers."

Collie would agree. "We don't know enough," she says. "We need money for research, money for education—both for the public and even the hospitals. Even the dumb pamphlet they gave me wasn't helpful. I didn't need one to explain what they had done; I needed them to say, 'You're not alone; there are miscarriage support groups in your area.'"

"The public needs information too," Collie continues. "My sister-in-law couldn't enjoy her pregnancy because several relatives had miscarriages. The fear kept her from even accepting a baby gift from me."

ABORTION

Another private grief is abortion. But not all of those babies were killed out of a selfish result of sin or because their parents found it inconvenient to bring another child into the world right then. In fact, I've met a number of women who live in quiet agony. They listen to their ministers decrying abortion; they hear testimonies of mothers who changed their minds about having the abortion and now point to their children with thankful pride. Many women sit quietly, their consciences twisting. Whenever they hear the battle cry "It's a myth to speak of 'therapeutic'—there's nothing therapeutic about it!" they keep seeing replays of their past and keep asking themselves questions such as: *Would I indeed have died if I'd gone through with that pregnancy, or was I conned by the medical profession? Why did my baby have to die anyway? Didn't I trust the Lord enough to see me through? What would my child be like today?*

RESIDENT PAIN

Many feel they can't fight boldly against abortions because someone might step out of the shadows, announcing the supposed hypocrisy. I remember one woman sobbing against my shoulder after I presented a grief seminar at her church. "How can I tell other people not to kill their babies when I killed mine?"

Awhile back, part of my grief seminar at a women's retreat in Michigan covered miscarriage and abortion. In the second half, I talked about how the Enemy loves to use guilt to hold us back from the emotional freedom and bright future that the Lord wants to give us. I noticed a timid-looking woman in the second row as she glanced up from her notebook to brush away tears. Inwardly, I said a quick prayer as I told the audience that people often come to counselors with unresolved issues even years after the death of a family member.

I glanced her way again just as she grimaced. I hurriedly stressed the security of 1 John 1:9. "If we confess our sins, he is faithful and just and will forgive us our sins and purify us from all unrighteousness." After confessing to God, we can ask that our message be relayed through prayer. A simple and sincere "And please tell my baby I'm sorry" helps.

At the seminar, I explained that in the mid-seventies, as many as 5 million American women were using intrauterine devices as their major contraceptive. Of those, between 1.5 and 2.2 million were using the newly developed Dalkon Shield, Copper T, and Cu-7 IUDs even though federal testing wasn't complete. In fact, the Copper T went on the market with the phrase "expected to receive FDA approval shortly."

The most severe complication from many of these IUDs was septic pregnancy, in which the rampant infection originating in the uterus rapidly spread to vital organs. Before widespread information was made available, eleven women had died—one of them in the same school district where I taught—and at least 209 others had been endangered. Because the septic-poisoning symptoms appeared suddenly, there was often little warning. One young mother died within thirty-one hours of the fever's onset.

I went on to explain that the Food and Drug Administration, Planned Parenthood, the manufacturers, and doctors were divided on what to do next. Some asked all patients using one of the three IUDs to consider having them removed. Still others took a wait-and-see position, saying the pill and pregnancy were greater threats. Only when the patient proved to be pregnant did some doctors remove the IUD, risking a spontaneous abortion. If the IUD was dislodged and they couldn't easily remove it, they recommended a hospital abortion.

A STATISTIC WITH A FACE

After the seminar, the woman from the second row approached me as I erased the board. Almost apologetically, she tipped her head as she looked up at me.

"I had a so-called 'therapeutic' abortion years ago."

"Tell me what happened" was all I had to say before the details tumbled out and the tears started down her cheeks again. The dislodged IUD with its copper elements threatened major problems, according to her doctor. He insisted she have an abortion, and within twenty-four hours, her pregnancy was terminated.

"Terminated!" she spat out the word. "They insisted I kill my baby, and they called it 'terminated.' I wasn't given any time to think about it, there were no options, and nobody told me I'd feel worse than if I'd gone ahead and taken the risk."

She found another tissue in her coat pocket before she continued. "I even went back to my doctor several months later, asking him to explain again why it had been so important that we rush. Know what he said? He said if I couldn't handle it, I should get some professional help. All I did was ask a simple question. Even these years later this hurts. What do I do?"

Even though the medical profession had said she didn't have a choice, she still felt if she'd trusted the Lord more, she wouldn't have submitted to the abortion. Her shoulders were slumped in defeat. She knew the medical reasons for the abortion, but she had a deeper need: forgiveness.

My questions to her were direct: Had she talked about this with the Lord? Yes. Did she accept the doctor's analysis that she had no other choice? No. Had she asked forgiveness from the Lord? Yes. Had she forgiven herself?

Tears sprang to her eyes. "No. How can I forgive myself for killing my baby?" she asked.

I put my arms around her. "First John 1:9 says, 'If we confess our sins, he is faithful and just and will forgive us our sins and purify us from all unrighteousness.' Please accept the Lord's forgiveness by forgiving yourself."

By then she was crying so hard there was nothing to do but pull her against my shoulder and pray that the Lord would let her feel His presence—and His freedom. At my amen she nodded her thanks, gave me a quick hug, and hurried out the door.

I watched her go, marveling that her shoulders seemed straighter. Maybe she understood she no longer had to be imprisoned by what had happened years ago. Maybe she was ready to accept God's forgiveness. Maybe she was even ready to forgive herself.

Abortion is a complex matter, and in standing against its vileness, we must not jump to conclusions about people's motives. Not every woman was trying to cover up sin. Some were blatantly misled. Whether the death occurs through miscarriage or through abortion, the child was a real child—not just a potential one. And for all grieving parents, God's gift of peace awaits.

Simple Reminders

1. Even though others were not aware of the existence of this child, the mother, especially, is often thrust into deep grief.

2. The miscarriage of this baby can taint the excitement of the next pregnancy because the parents know what can happen.

3. The husband's way of coping is usually to shut down emotionally. Women often need to talk about it and talk about it.

4. Even if a friend just sits and nods with the grieving mother, she is helping.

5. Not all aborted babies were killed out of a selfish result of sin or because their parents found it inconvenient to bring another child into the world right then.

12 Sound Financial Decisions in the Midst of Grief

So, What Do I Do with the Insurance Money?

Before Don died, I'd never balanced the checkbook or even read—let alone understood—the income tax papers he asked me to sign. When his death catapulted me into financial decision making, I was terrified my mistakes would rob Jay and Holly of the education we'd planned and force me into pushing a rusted shopping cart—piled with my books and quilts—through the streets of Detroit.

Don had wisecracked to friends he was worth more dead than alive, so, after his death, word got around that he had left me "very well off." To correct that wrong assumption seemed disloyal, so I walked a scary, lonesome path as I learned to protect what I did have. I can think of at least ninety-seven things I'd rather do than read

139

about budgets and savings accounts, but I timidly began my journey by studying the financial-planning articles in the women's magazines. At least none of the printed pages would say, "I can't believe you have a master's degree and don't know this." Gradually I discovered the investment section in the local library.

Now I have a number of good investment books on my bookshelf, but it still took me awhile to wade through that unfamiliar territory. Gradually, though, I learned about pensions, mortgage equity, and interest rates. And, to my great amazement, I eventually started my own business, Bold Words, Inc., and learned about business finances. So, believe me, if I can learn all this stuff, it should be a snap for anyone else. But while I was wading through all those personal budget books early in my singlehood, I came up with five money-management rules I now emphasize when I'm asked to speak on finances at grief seminars:

- Don't do anything without praying for guidance.
- Don't make any major changes for the first year.
- Get a good lawyer.
- Get a good tax accountant.
- Don't let the relatives borrow money.

PRAY FOR GUIDANCE

Real security comes from the Lord—not from even the wisest of earthly investments. And even if we manage to gather great wealth, we are merely stewards of His property. I was well aware of the responsibilities I had for the care of my children—who are now grown—and I still take 1 Timothy 5:8 seriously: "If anyone does not provide for his relatives, and especially for his immediate family, he has denied the faith and is worse than an unbeliever." But learning how to best provide for my children didn't happen overnight.

My B.A. and M.A. degrees are from Eastern Michigan University, but I've often said my "Ph.D." is from the School of Hard Knocks. Even before I became a widow, I'd already learned to pray about any major decision for three days. Financially, that translates into "If anybody's pressing for an immediate answer, run!"

Some folks believe it's too "worldly" to be concerned about financial matters and even say money is evil. But 1 Timothy 6:10 says, "The *love* of money is the root of all evil" (KJV, emphasis added)—not money itself. Money is inanimate; how it's used is what matters.

Tithing is one way to make sure the money is put to good use. I realize the tithe is based on Old Testament practice rather than New Testament command, but I like giving to God's work. I can't go to Ethiopia or Bolivia, but I can help others go. And I still get to be part of what God is doing for eternity.

Often I hear people say so many groups ask for money they don't know who to send it to. Here's an easy rule: Support only those missionaries or organizations you know or have studied. If you don't know the group well but feel as though the Lord is nudging you that way, do your homework. Ask other Christians what they know about the group, send for their annual report, and call the Better Business Bureau near their headquarters to see if they have any complaints against them. If the organization is national or international in its ministry, contact the Evangelical Council for Financial Accountability and ask if the organization is a member in good standing. And as you're asking for the Lord's guidance, determine to follow it.

I remember Karen's husband, James, who always seemed to be trading cars. When he wanted to buy a secondhand yellow sedan they couldn't afford, Karen insisted they pray about the purchase for three days first. James assented but, without Karen's knowledge, verbally agreed to buy the car and had the dealership hold it for him. Less than three months later, the transmission went out, resulting in a massive repair bill. To Karen's credit, she didn't say, "I told you so," even as her husband guiltily confessed his past deception and present conviction that the Lord would have spared them the hassle if only he had listened.

As you are asking for guidance, take comfort in the thought the Lord won't tell you anything in prayer that contradicts His Word, including urging you to grab a get-rich-quick scheme. Proverbs 21:5 says, "The plans of the diligent lead to profit as surely as haste leads to poverty." Just a few chapters later, Proverbs 28:22 says, "A stingy man is eager to get rich and is unaware that poverty awaits him."

Being good stewards of God's money means that we put it to good use—even if that's no more than allowing it to accumulate interest in a savings account—and not foolishly risk it through "sure-fire" schemes.

If the thought of being a good steward for its own sake isn't persuasive enough, may I remind you that by taking care of the insurance money we not only keep from becoming a burden to our children but can, in fact, leave an inheritance. Proverbs 13:22 says, "A good man leaves an inheritance for his children's children." And that goes for a "good woman" too.

WAIT A YEAR BEFORE MAKING ANY MAJOR CHANGES

Stress does awful things even to the most logical mind. But selling everything and running away, even under the guise of a new beginning, complicates the emotional healing. Knowing that Jay and Holly needed the stability only I could provide kept me from taking the next plane out of Michigan on the rough days. Even though the memory of their dad was in every corner of our home, being able to stay in familiar rooms helped us deal with our grief. During the next three years, the lack of upheaval helped them accumulate the emotional strength they'd need when we did move.

The second good thing I did was to keep our summer place for four more years. Within a month after Don's death, I received numerous offers, but I was determined to hang on to it as long as I was financially able. Not only were most of our friends there, but that was the only place Jay and Holly could remember being in the summer. When I had to sell it later, I had realized it wasn't the place itself I wanted, but Don and those lost years. By then, our children were older and were comfortable with doing other things during the summer.

Because I remembered the way the illogical seemed logical during that awful first year of grief, I've tried to caution others against making major decisions in those early months after a trauma. Then one summer, a cousin died from complications after giving birth to her fourth child. (Yes, that still happens today.)

Her husband gave us a new understanding of the phrase "wild with grief" as he announced he couldn't properly care for another baby and gave her up for adoption. Several women, including his own mother, offered to care for the child until he could work through his pain, but his mind was set. Besides, he said, it wasn't fair to the child to let this drag on. He insisted upon signing the legal papers and "getting on with life."

You know how this story ends. Yep, six months later, he was sitting in a lawyer's office, tearfully demanding help in getting his daughter back. But the state law was unforgiving and provided no loopholes despite his grief.

GET A GOOD LAWYER

Statistics tell us that between 65 to 80 percent of the population do not have a will. Some think they have plenty of time, some have gotten it into their heads they're going to live forever, and still others are afraid they'll create a self-fulfilling prophecy. After all, if you have a will drawn up, you might need it!

I hate to be the one to tell you this, friend, but death is *not* optional. If the Lord tarries, *all* of us are going to close our eyes here and open them in eternity.

Don and I had always had a handwritten will and even had it witnessed by friends. But Don had taught business law for years and knew the safest documents were the official ones. Within a week after his release from the hospital after that first cancer diagnosis, he made a call to his school district administration office asking for their recommendation of a local attorney who was a member "in good standing" of the American Bar Association. The resulting appointment took less than an hour, but Don had done everything he could to make sure the property transfers would be done as effortlessly as possible and without extensive delays. I'll always be grateful for his thoughtfulness.

Too many folks think, *Well that's fine for people with property, but I don't own enough to go to all the trouble of doing a will.* Do you own more than the shirt on your back? Do you have a savings account? A checking account? Savings bonds? A gold watch that belonged to your father? If so, you want to have a say in how those things are distributed after your death.

144

And you can't assume that everything will automatically go to the spouse. Since laws vary from state to state, the worse assumption anyone can make is that the government will do things the way the individual had hoped. In many states, without a will stating otherwise, the wife receives only one-third to one-half of her husband's estate—even if her income purchased the property—and the rest will go to the children. She will have to keep actual accounts of how she provides for the minors in her care and has no voice in how they spend their portion of the money once they reach legal age.

No will may mean the living expenses will force her to sell the family home, even if it was purchased with money from an earlier inheritance from her parents. And without a will, any distant relative can come swooping in with a claim against the estate, further tying up the proceedings.

Of course lawyers aren't cheap, but they can save us money and hassle later. And many of them donate their services in the evening for those who truly can't afford to have wills drawn up. A call to your local social-services agency will let you know where that's available.

Part of the procedure requires that you provide your lawyer with a list of assets—naming your mortgage holder, insurance agent, savings- and checking-account numbers, pension holder, and any investments you or your children have. If nothing else, the list will convince you that you have more assets than you thought.

One of the paragraphs in the will calls for the naming of an executor—someone to take care of the financial details after the death. Choosing that person is harder than deciding who gets the savings account and the heirlooms. Who should that person be? A relative? Your lawyer?

Since every situation is different, I can't offer hard-and-fast rules.

But I do suggest that you know the person well. Is this person capable of handling details over several months? Notice, I'm not asking how much you love him or her, just how well the person is going to function under financial pressure. Will this person give in to family members who feel as though they were treated unfairly?

Wills should change as circumstances change. While Jay and Holly were still minors, I tried to anticipate all the problems they'd be faced with if I died suddenly, so I wanted guardians who had enough energy to guide them through the turbulent high-school years. The ones who best fit that description were Carl and Marilyn, close friends who, I like to say, knew Jay and Holly five years *before* they were born. Our situation then was further complicated: Carl and Marilyn were living in Michigan, while we were living in New York. Thus, I had two executors. My local lawyer, whom I accepted through the recommendation of dear friends, would have handled the selling of our townhouse and transferred the resulting funds to the Michigan bank handling the details of Jay's and Holly's educations. From there, Carl and Marilyn would have taken over.

I was obviously trusting that the Lord would allow me to see my children safely into adulthood—and He has done exactly that—but I had learned even then that God doesn't always do things our way. By anticipating the things that *could* happen, I freed myself from worry that a judge might appoint someone as guardian who might not be a good choice for my children.

GET A GOOD TAX ACCOUNTANT

Don't let a relative, including your own brother, handle your taxes unless he's a certified public accountant (CPA) and has always done them for you. Widows are especially vulnerable because most of our husbands handled the financial decisions. Our fears make us only too eager to turn financial responsibilities over to someone else again. Don't do it. Even as you ask for counsel, do your own homework and learn all you can about the decisions only you should be making. And keep praying.

After Don's death, our lawyer asked who did our tax preparations. When I answered, "Don," he recommended the accountants who handled his own business records and insisted I make an immediate appointment.

In that first call to the CPA, I heard words I only vaguely remembered Don using—"tax liability," "deductions," "adjusted gross income." Then he asked that I bring copies of our tax returns for the past five years to his office.

Copies of tax returns? Where on earth would Don have put those? I looked in all the usual places, including his filing cabinet that I had taken over for my writing assignments. Nothing. Next I looked in all of the illogical places, finally cleaning out every drawer in our bedroom. Still nothing.

After three hours of searching every drawer on both floors, I could think of nothing else to do except call my teaching buddy, Carl.

"How do I get copies from the IRS?" I asked. "Don must have thrown ours out. You know how he hated clutter."

Carl chuckled. "Ah, come on. He was a business teacher. There's no way he would have thrown them out. They're in that house someplace. If you don't find them soon, Marilyn and I will come over and help you look."

After I hung up the phone, I remained seated, leaning my head against the spot where my beloved Scotsman had rested his. "Donnie, *where* are those papers?" I asked, then waited for his laughing retort, but only the January wind answered.

I tried again. "Donnie, you always handled the taxes. Where are those copies?" Still only silence.

How was I going to survive widowhood if I couldn't find five lousy tax copies? I leaned forward, my hands covering my face. "Lord, you've promised to supply all my needs. Well, I need those tax papers, and I've looked everywhere. Please tell me where they are."

Even before I could say amen, the image of a brown briefcase sitting under the basement steps came to mind. We'd moved the filing cabinet up to my office on the second floor several months ago but hadn't gotten around to taking all the files. I bounded down the steps and grabbed the briefcase. Of course, it was filled with tax papers.

As I counted out the needed copies, I thought of my having asked Don just a few minutes earlier to tell me where they were. I'd been talking to the wrong person. It wasn't until I'd prayed and asked for the Lord's help that I remembered the briefcase.

I quickly gathered the copies for 1976–81 but still searched through all the papers, looking for—what? Perhaps a letter from Don to encourage me. How I would have loved to have found a note in his bold handwriting, saying, "You *can* do this, San." But nothing but tax papers were in the case. I was still very much on my own.

Don had kept only the essential records each tax year, but I was terrified someone official would demand to see every receipt. Thus, for the first few years, I kept everything—even labeling a box "Important papers that I don't know what to do with." Now I've finally culled out the unnecessary and made room for the rest.

Along the way, I've learned I don't have to keep canceled checks or tax returns more than six years old, receipts for items I no longer own, bank statements more than a year old, monthly missions receipts (I need only the annual receipt), or receipts more than six months old for utilities. Not keeping everything eliminates massive clutter.

Awhile back, I was in one of those classic cleaning moods and discovered a cardboard box of canceled checks from the late sixties, when we were still newlyweds. It took me several evenings to sort through all those years of checks, but I wanted to keep the ones marking milestones—for our first home, for graduate school, for Jay's and Holly's deliveries. Letting go is never easy, so of course all those checks in Don's handwriting triggered countless memories. But keeping those pieces of paper hadn't brought him back, and I finally ran most of the checks through the shredder without another thought.

REFRAIN FROM LENDING MONEY TO THE RELATIVES

You are not a bank—even though your extended family may treat you like one. That's another advantage to putting any insurance check immediately into certificates of deposit; you can't get at the money after hearing all those sad stories. If you ignore the first part of this rule—"Don't let the relatives borrow money"—please listen to the second part: "But if you do, make sure you have them sign a note."

Karen's sister and brother-in-law had struggled financially since the beginning of their marriage and were snared into thinking they could buy everything they wanted now and just pay it off gradually while they enjoyed it. By the time Karen received the settlement from her husband's estate, her sister, brother-in-law, and two young toddlers were living in his mother's unfinished basement, unable to handle the town's rising rents along with their credit-card balances.

When they found a small house they could afford, they didn't have the money for a down payment. Would Karen help them get their children out of the basement? Of course.

Several months later, as Karen met with the accountant preparing her income-tax return, this information came out. The accountant was adamant that she get a signed note. Karen was hurt. "But she's my sister," she replied.

"I don't care," he retorted. "You get that note. Tell them I insisted you have to have it for income-tax purposes. Tell them I yelled at you. Just get it."

Reluctantly Karen did exactly that, apologizing all the while. A year later, she was thanking the accountant for his foresight—her sister and husband were in the process of an ugly divorce, and that signed note was pivotal in his releasing his rights to the house. He said if his ex-wife would pay off the note, he'd sign off on the house, and she wouldn't have to sell it. Their two children could remain in their home instead of living in someone else's basement again.

Perhaps you won't be asked for thousands of dollars, but just for a "few hundred." Giving adult children money out of a misplaced sense of responsibility, or even out of guilt, does them no favors—nor are you "denying your faith" if you choose not to give it to them (see 1 Timothy 5:8). Sometimes we best provide for our families by saying no. But if you do decide you'd rather let them have the money than worry about not letting them have it, chalk it up mentally as a gift. That way, if you decide you'll never see the money again, at least you won't be disappointed when they don't repay you.

If you think I'm being harsh, let me end with an all-too-familiar true story. One of my friends lives in a senior citizen's mobile-home complex. Each year their neighborhood sees three or four new widows created, most of whom are bewildered by the financial decisions swooping down upon them. One widow decided she'd solve her problems by putting her house and her money in her son's name, thereby relieving her of any decision making.

Poor choice. The son got into financial trouble and sold her home! As of this writing, his mother doesn't have an idea of where she's going to live or what she'll do for the rest of her life. And all because she was afraid of learning to manage her own money.

Because I am God's child, He is concerned about every aspect of my life. I like the three verbs in Luke 11:9: "*Ask* and it will be given to you; *seek* and you will find; *knock* and the door will be opened to you" (emphasis added). Asking, seeking, and knocking are words of *our* action. Even as much as we long to be rescued from problems, we still are responsible for the results. The Lord has promised to help us, but we have to do our part too.

Simple Reminders

1. Don't do anything without praying for guidance. Real security comes from the Lord and not from even the best earthly investments.

2. Don't make any major changes for the first year. Like it or not, we aren't thinking clearly.

3. Get a good lawyer. You can't assume that everything automatically will go to whom you want.

4. Get a good tax accountant. Widows especially are vulnerable because most husbands handle the financial matters.

5. Don't let the relatives borrow money. But if you do, make sure they sign a note if you ever want to see the money again.

$1\mathcal{3}$ *Facing the Future*

Yes, You Will Smile Again

My Kentucky grandmother used to say, "Honey, there are some things in life that all you can do with 'em is bear 'em." But "bearing" them is easier if we can make some sense of the tragedy.

Go Forward

Philippians 4:19 was the scripture ten-year-old Jay was memorizing the day his dad died. The copied verse from the King James Version was on the kitchen counter when I came home from the hospital to tell the children the bad news. The note paper almost seemed to glow, as though the Lord Himself was offering special comfort: "But my God shall supply all your need according to his riches in glory by Christ Jesus."

Many times I tested that promise, even occasionally challenging Him with "Even this need, God?" Gradually I learned that He hadn't overlooked anything. Amazingly I learned to do many of the things that had belonged to Don's traditional role—even changing the oil in the car and balancing the checkbook. But most of all I grew, learning much about myself and even more about my heavenly Father.

COUNT THE BLESSINGS

During the early months after Don's death, I felt as though my prayers weren't going anywhere. I was still talking to God, but I wasn't hearing answers the way I had during Don's struggle. Feeling spiritually abandoned, I demanded, "Why aren't You talking to me?"

Suddenly I thought of times when I had held an injured Jay or Holly on my lap. I hadn't talked but had merely held them against my heart, surrounding their hurt with my love. As I cried out, I realized that was what the Lord was now doing for me. I was too hurt to listen to His plans for the future. I was capable of receiving only His comfort for that moment. In time, He would ease me off His lap and tenderly lead me to the tasks He planned. His silence hadn't meant He'd stopped caring.

During the early weeks of our grief, I was determined that while Jay and Holly had lost their dad physically, they weren't going to lose me emotionally. Every night as I tucked them in bed, I asked if they wanted to talk before we prayed together. Sometimes Jay shared a special memory of his dad or had a question about something at the funeral home. But not Holly. She still hadn't cried and kept all of her searing questions inside. As she prayed, her words were rote instead of from the heart.

154

Even as I continued to ask if she wanted to talk, she'd shake her head and turn away. Then one night, about two weeks after the funeral, she paused, then said, "I do wonder about one thing: When we prayed, didn't God listen?"

Oh, boy. With that one question, she'd galloped to the universal heart's cry.

Mentally I shot a quick prayer for calmness and fresh ideas and then began the hardest explanation I've ever tried to give. We all compare ourselves to others; the trick is to get that comparison going in the right direction.

I reminded her of my Grandpa Ted who had died after his leg was severed in a Kentucky coal mine. He had been only twenty-two years old and had left three children under the age of four. I reminded her of a twenty-eight-year-old man who had been killed at the corner just the week before. His wife was pregnant with a child he would never hold. Then I talked about God's gift to us of those extra sixteen months when the doctors thought her daddy would die within weeks. I added that he could have died with the first cancer when she had been only three years old.

When I was talked out, I asked if she felt like praying that night. She nodded, then began, "Thank you, God, that Daddy died now instead of when I was little."

I didn't hear much of the rest of her prayer. She was only eight years old.

LEARN SELF-CARE

Both 1 Corinthians 3:16 and 6:19 proclaim that our bodies are temples of God's Holy Spirit. We've all heard the sermons that we, therefore, aren't to destroy that temple by smoking, drinking, committing adultery, or overeating. But we can also destroy the temple by not resting, exercising, or eating properly.

While we're learning to take care of ourselves, some grievers resume abandoned hobbies. Others begin developing healthy habits. That's an area I'm still trying to work on. Walking helps me. During the spring and summer, I have no trouble getting up at 5:00 A.M. to walk for two miles. But the winter months pose another problem. Since walking is enjoyable only when I can see the interesting things around me, I had to find other ways, such as walking at noon, to get that trek in.

It's also important to keep in close communication with the Lord, so regrets and sins don't build up. Proverbs 28:13 says, "He who conceals his sins does not prosper, but whoever confesses and renounces them finds mercy." Confession really is good for the soul.

Quite often when I speak, women tell me amazing things afterward. I used to think they were convinced I had answers just because I had the nerve to speak in front of a group. But now I think they need someplace to dump the hurts they carry. I've prayed with women struggling with guilt for their own sins as well as for those who were sinned against through incest, alcoholic parents, lonely childhoods, taunting relatives, constant moves, poverty, whatever. The stories never become stale because each one carries fresh suffering.

After we pray, I suggest they tell someone who can help them work through the various issues. Of course only the Lord can heal, but sometimes people are so hurt they need help hearing His voice.

HELP OTHERS

Matthew 7:12 states, "In everything, do to others what you would have them do to you, for this sums up the Law and the Prophets."

So as that first Christmas after Don's death loomed, I remembered our positive experience the previous month of serving the Thanksgiving meal at the Salvation Army. Time to make another call. The staff welcomed our help in delivering food baskets to the elderly or ill. But the morning of our assignment was so cold I couldn't get warm even with my new coat tightly buttoned against the wind.

Our first delivery was up a set of rickety steps to an apartment over a downtown store. An elderly woman opened the door cautiously, waiting for me to identify myself. Her eyes settled immediately upon the red Salvation Army badge pinned to my coat collar. Then she grinned as she saw Jay and Holly smiling at her.

She started to speak but instead cleared her throat several times as though she wasn't used to talking. Finally she gestured to the table in the middle of the one room that served as living room, bedroom, and kitchen. I unpacked the small turkey, potatoes, canned green beans, cranberry sauce, and rolls.

"Is all this for me?" she finally managed to ask. "Are you sure they haven't made a mistake? Why, this is a feast!" Her eyes sparkled as she looked at the food heaped on the small table.

I wondered how long it had been since that stark room had heard so many words.

"Oh, I know there's no mistake," I said. "The social services director gave me your name himself."

Her aged face crinkled into a grin.

We said our good-byes, and I went out the door a bit happier than when I had climbed those dark stairs. The next stops were to weather-beaten houses and more one-room apartments. We three carried in the bags, stayed momentarily to hear about grandchildren who looked like Jay and Holly, and heard excuses why adult children couldn't visit over the holidays. A "Merry Christmas" was said along with each good-bye, but I still wasn't any closer to peace. I was cold, the weather was miserable, and I couldn't see that I was making a great difference in anyone's life. If we hadn't been delivering the groceries, someone else would have.

The last address was several miles south. Watching the snow swirl across the road, I started the car. The sooner we made this last delivery, the sooner we could go home. Some intangible wind cut through even the closely woven fibers of my new coat.

Jay and Holly were almost asleep by the time we reached the area. I steered with my left hand and groped for the address card. Glancing at the back, I noticed handwritten words under the category "Special Needs." That space had been blank on the other cards, but this one plainly stated, "Large-size woman's coat."

I wished I'd seen that before we left. I could have chosen a coat off the rack against the back wall. With the rush of the holidays, no one else from the Salvation Army would make a special trip way out there just to deliver a coat. And I certainly wasn't going to offer my own on such a cold afternoon, even though I wore the same size.

At last we arrived at the address on the card. Years ago, the place must have been a cute cottage. Now it was only a tired, leaning shack. Its graying boards still showed signs of white paint, undoubtedly applied many years ago. An old car sat in the yard—up on blocks and tireless. I wondered if they had sold the tires to provide something else they needed.

As I shut off the ignition, Jay and Holly sat up and looked around. "Gosh, Mom," was Jay's only comment as he saw the house.

As we walked toward the front door, an elderly woman at the window solemnly gestured toward the back. The front door was sealed with plastic to keep out December's sub-zero temperatures.

The three of us stamped our feet at the back steps as a man in his seventies held the door for us. "Don't worry about the snow," he said. But still we stamped, perhaps stalling for time.

Once inside, I set the bag on the kitchen table, trying not to notice the worn-out room. Everything was clean, but only near the walls were pieces of tile left. Those once in the middle of the room had been worn to the floorboards beneath. The curtains had been mended so many times the stitches made a pattern in the flimsy material.

The elderly couple thanked me repeatedly. All I had to do was smile and walk out the door. Instead, I found myself apologizing for not having brought a coat. The woman smoothed the sleeves of her old navy blue sweater and gave us an "it's okay" smile.

It struck me she'd been disappointed so many times that another disappointment hardly mattered. Through the curtains I could see the snow blowing across the frozen driveway. Suddenly I took off my coat and said, "Here, try this one on for size."

She hesitated, then did as I asked. She even buttoned it and smiled at her husband as she turned to show him the back. It fit! I leaned forward to unpin the badge from the collar.

"Looks like you got yourself a coat," I stammered, afraid she wouldn't accept.

Instead, she hugged me and whispered, "God bless you, honey," as tears rolled down her cheeks.

Suddenly I was crying too. What had been awkwardly offered was graciously accepted.

"Thank you for letting me do this," I whispered.

Her husband and Jay and Holly silently watched, not sure what to do. Soon we were out the door, waving good-bye to the old couple standing together.

As soon as the door closed, Holly turned to me. "Mom! It's freezing! And you gave away your coat!"

I felt like giggling. "I know. Isn't it wonderful? Nobody needs two gray coats anyway. And you know what? This is the warmest I've been all day."

I gave Holly's shoulders a squeeze. Hysteria wouldn't threaten me again for a long time.

TAKE THE GOOD FROM THE PAST INTO THE FUTURE

Second Corinthians 1:3–4 reads, "Praise be to the God and Father of our Lord Jesus Christ, the Father of compassion and the God of all comfort, who comforts us in all our troubles, so that we can comfort those in any trouble with the comfort we ourselves have received from God."

In Genesis 50:20, Joseph says as he talks to his brothers in Egypt, years after they had sold him to a caravan, "You intended to harm me, but God intended it for good to accomplish what is now being done, the saving of many lives."

I am convinced that God can—and will—bring His good out of any situation we give to Him.

I was reminded of that truth again the morning I was thrust into the unfamiliar world of tire-buying. Don had always taken care of the car's maintenance, so I ignored the balding tires. Then a blowout on the expressway forced me to deal with the issue. The next morning I was in the tire shop, nodding at what I thought were the appropriate times as the salesman explained threads and radials, Ls and Ks. The strain surely showed on my face.

"Why don't you grab a cup of coffee next door while we put the new tires on?" the young man suggested.

Once I was in the sunshine, the tears ran down my face. "Okay, God," I muttered. "I hate it that I'm having to do this. I hate it that Don's dead. He should be helping me raise Jay and Holly. He should be making decisions about the car. I want some encouragement right now!"

I swiped at my eyes and turned toward the coffee shop. A young woman was standing by the open hood of her car. As I asked if she needed help, she insisted it would start again in another ten minutes—after it cooled off a bit. So we pushed it out of the way, and I invited her to have a cup of coffee with me.

Over the steaming cups, we made small talk. She asked if I was married. When I told her Don had died just a few months before, I expected her to mutter, "Oh, I'm sorry."

Instead, she shrugged. "How long were you married?"

"Sixteen and a half years."

She took a sip of her coffee. "Did you love him?"

"Yes, very much."

"Did he love you?"

I smiled. "Oh, yes."

Again she shrugged. "Then you've already experienced more love than most of us. Think of that instead of what you've lost."

Then she told about her divorce—the beatings, the custody battles, the continuing threats. Suddenly she looked at her watch. "Hey, I gotta go to work. But thanks for listening. That helped a lot."

She was out the door before I could tell her how much *she* had helped me. God had certainly answered my prayer for encouragement, but not at all in the way I had expected.

GET TO KNOW YOURSELF BETTER

Don't be afraid of the quietness of your home. Don't go running from place to place, but give yourself time to discover who you really are. And let each day shine! I love going for walks, especially on crisp days. But I always look for something unusual, such as a red-leafed tree against a blue sky or orange and red bittersweet clinging to a tree limb.

During one of my trips in which I noticed marvel after marvel, I was frustrated by not being able to share the adventure with Don. Then one night I dreamed he was standing by my bed, laughing his unabashed belly laugh. "Ah, San," he said, "you're going to discover that I never really died."

And that's true. His death taught me the value of laughter and the preciousness of *this* day. Now I cling to the Lord and try not to give in to the pain of the loss. This world is not the end. I will see my beloved clown again. And may we all be able to cling to that biblical hope.

Simple Reminders

1. Often we don't hear the Lord during our grief, but it helps to know that He is holding us close to His heart, surrounding us with His love.

2. Learning to take care of ourselves in the midst of grief can be both a challenge and a new beginning.

3. Find ways to help others and thus help yourself.

4. It helps to know that God can bring His good out of any situation given to Him.

5. Get to know yourself better during your grief.

6. Knowing that we will see our loved ones again is a wonderful biblical principle to which we can cling.

Study Guide

Chapter 1. Clowns Aren't Supposed to Die

1. Which special person have you lost to death? What were the circumstances?

2. Did the death of that special person raise any theological questions for you? If so, what were they?

3. Have you ever been thrust into a role-reversal situation?

4. Have people ever expected you to be stronger than you are?

5. Was there anything your ill friend or family member wanted to see completed?

6. Would your life be changed if you prayed to bear the pain—whether physical or emotional—rather than for it to be removed?

CHAPTER 2. "DONNIE, YOU'RE FREE!"

1. Have you ever refused to face the truth about a physical condition? What was the situation?

2. Have you ever faced a situation that demanded more emotional strength than you thought you were capable of?

3. Have you ever felt God's presence in a tangible way? What happened?

4. Have you ever had to say, "Your will only, Lord." If so, when?

CHAPTER 3. UNDERSTANDING GRIEF

1. How many grief prompters—intense relationship, sudden, premature, violent—have you experienced?

2. Have you ever experienced anticipatory grief? If so, when?

3. In what ways have you participated in God's bringing good out of your pain?

4. Have you faced your own mortality? If so, how did this come about?

CHAPTER 4. MOVING THROUGH THE GRIEF

1. Have you experienced the grief stages? If so, which ones were the most challenging?

2. Did you experience physical symptoms during an emotional crisis? If so, what were they?

3. Has anyone tried to tell you how you must grieve?

4. What incident signaled to you that you were moving forward in grief?

5. Unfortunately, guilt is a normal part of grief. Have you struggled in this area?

CHAPTER 5. SURVIVING THE LOSS

1. Have you ever hesitated to approach God because you knew your attitude needed work?

2. Do you struggle with being kind to yourself? If so, what helps?

3. How do you handle threatening tears?

4. Have you ever supplied the right action toward another and then found that forgiveness followed?

CHAPTER 6. HOW TO HELP OTHERS

1. Have you ever felt as though you had to "put on a happy face" despite your grief?

2. Have you ever wanted to hurry along your grief or that of another? What happened?

3. What practical help have you received or offered during bereavement?

4. Have you known anyone who started dating too soon after the death of a spouse? What happened?

5. What important dates do you wish people would remember with you?

CHAPTER 7. TALKING WITH A CHILD ABOUT DEATH

1. What was your earliest introduction to death? Did anyone help you understand what was happening?

2. What do you wish adults had done differently for you during that time?

3. What are your thoughts on allowing children to attend a funeral?

4. Have you ever been introduced to a new helpful thought about death by a child? If so, what was it?

5. In what ways do you see adults reaching out to children during hurtful times? In what ways would you like to see improvement?

CHAPTER 8. ABNORMAL GRIEF

1. Are you comfortable sharing how you cope with grief?

2. What do you think would be the most effective way to help someone who is struggling with chronic grief?

3. Have you encountered someone who displayed extraordinary acceptance of the tragedy at the time but then had a delayed reaction? What happened?

4. What examples of avoidance and denial as coping mechanisms have you witnessed?

CHAPTER 9. COPING WITH NORMAL DEPRESSION

1. What experience have you had with those who are depressed?

2. Have you known of depression causing physical problems? What was the situation?

3. Do you think it's possible to ward off normal depression in the face of life's challenges?

4. What effect does depression have on the family of the one dealing with it?

CHAPTER 10. COPING WITH THE DEATH OF A CHILD

1. What has been your experience with the death of a child?

2. What have you found to be the most helpful activity for grieving parents?

3. What would you suggest for those who want to help grieving parents?

4. How would you suggest grieving parents handle the holidays?

5. How do you react when you hear about the death of a child?

CHAPTER 11. THOUGHTS ON MISCARRIAGE AND ABORTION

1. What is your earliest memory of someone who had either a miscarriage or an abortion?

2. How was the situation handled by the others involved?

3. How would you have liked for the situation to have been handled?

4. What do you think is most helpful for parents who have miscarried?

5. What do you think is most helpful for parents who have aborted their child?

Chapter 12. Sound Financial Decisions in the Midst of Grief

1. What financial challenges have you seen created by the death of a spouse?

2. What financial advice do you have for widows? Widowers?

3. Have you ever prayed about missing papers? What happened?

4. Have you ever tried to bail someone out of a financial mess? Would you handle the situation differently today? If so, how?

5. How can the church help with financial decisions in the early months of grief?

Chapter 13. Facing the Future

1. Have you ever felt abandoned by God during deep grief? What happened to make you feel this way?

2. What was your greatest challenge in learning to take care of your own needs while grieving?

3. Have you seen God bring His good out of a tragic situation? If so, what was the result?

4. What were some of the things you learned about yourself during a painful grief process?

5. Whom are you looking forward to seeing again?

Notes

Chapter 4. Moving through the Grief

1. Elisabeth Kubler-Ross, *On Death and Dying* (New York: Macmillian Publishing Co., 1970).

Chapter 6. How to Help Others

1. William H. Frey II, Ph.D., and Muriel Langseth, *Crying: The Mystery of Tears* (San Francisco: Harper, 1985).

Chapter 10. Coping with the Death of a Child

1. Rebecca Faber, *A Mother's Grief Observed* (Wheaton, Ill.: Tyndale Publishing House, 1997), 78.

2. For more information about The Compassionate Friends, check your local white pages or contact their headquarters at P. O. Box 3696, Oak Brook, Illinois 60522-3696; (630)990–0010.